DIGITAL DISRUPTION AND ELECTRONIC RESOURCE MANAGEMENT IN LIBRARIES

CHANDOS
INFORMATION PROFESSIONAL SERIES
Series Editor: Ruth Rikowski
(email: Rikowskigr@aol.com)

Chandos' new series of books is aimed at the busy information professional. They have been specially commissioned to provide the reader with an authoritative view of current thinking. They are designed to provide easy-to-read and (most importantly) practical coverage of topics that are of interest to librarians and other information professionals. If you would like a full listing of current and forthcoming titles, please visit www.chandospublishing.com.

New authors: we are always pleased to receive ideas for new titles; if you would like to write a book for Chandos, please contact Dr Glyn Jones on g.jones.2@elsevier.com or telephone +44 (0) 1865 843000

DIGITAL DISRUPTION AND ELECTRONIC RESOURCE MANAGEMENT IN LIBRARIES

NIHAR K. PATRA

ELSEVIER

CHANDOS
PUBLISHING
An imprint of Elsevier • elsevier.com

Chandos Publishing is an imprint of Elsevier
50 Hampshire Street, 5th Floor, Cambridge, MA 02139, United States
The Boulevard, Langford Lane, Kidlington, OX5 1GB, United Kingdom

Notices

Knowledge and best practice in this field are constantly changing. As new research and experience broaden our understanding, changes in research methods, professional practices, or medical treatment may become necessary.

Practitioners and researchers must always rely on their own experience and knowledge in evaluating and using any information, methods, compounds, or experiments described herein. In using such information or methods they should be mindful of their own safety and the safety of others, including parties for whom they have a professional responsibility.

To the fullest extent of the law, neither the Publisher nor the authors, contributors, or editors, assume any liability for any injury and/or damage to persons or property as a matter of products liability, negligence or otherwise, or from any use or operation of any methods, products, instructions, or ideas contained in the material herein.

ISBN: 978-0-08-102045-6 (print)
ISBN: 978-0-08-102046-3 (online)

British Library Cataloguing-in-Publication Data
A catalogue record for this book is available from the British Library

Library of Congress Cataloging-in-Publication Data
A catalog record for this book is available from the Library of Congress

For information on all Chandos Publishing visit our
website at https://www.elsevier.com/books-and-journals

Working together
to grow libraries in
developing countries

www.elsevier.com • www.bookaid.org

Publisher: Glyn Jones
Acquisition Editor: George Knott
Editorial Project Manager: Lindsay Lawrence
Production Project Manager: Omer Mukthar
Designer: Mark Rogers

Typeset by MPS Limited, Chennai, India

DEDICATION

For my wife, Niharika, and newborn baby boy, Adideva.
Thank you for all your love and support—Nihar K. Patra.

CONTENTS

LIST OF FIGURES

LIST OF TABLES

BIOGRAPHY

Dr. Nihar K. Patra has over 16 years of experience in the library profession, with substantial experience in using the latest IT infrastructure in libraries, including the development of a Digital Library, Web-based Information Services, Library Portal Development, and RFID. He was awarded a PhD degree, and also completed his MPhil degree in Library and Information Science. Dr. Nihar K. Patra is presently working at Nalanda University as University Librarian. Nalanda University, an international institute of national importance established by a special Act of Indian Parliament, i.e., The Nalanda University Act 2010, is an International Institution of Excellence for the pursuit of intellectual, philosophical, historical, and spiritual studies. Being a young University Librarian, his present job calls for the development and complete revival of the Nalanda International University Library from scratch.

Prior to his present assignment, Dr. Nihar K. Patra was associated with NIFTEM (the National Institute of Food Technology Entrepreneurship and Management), Ministry of Food Processing Industries (MoFPI), government of India, where he set up a world-class state-of-the-art library through the implementation of the latest IT infrastructure. He has had the privilege of being associated with the libraries of some of the elite institutes in India, such as JK Lakshmipat University; NSHM Knowledge Campus, Kolkata; Xavier Labour Relation Institute (XLRI), Jamshedpur; Indian Institute for Production Management (IIPM), Kansbahal; National Institute of Fashion Technology (NIFT), Gandhinagar; Institute for Plasma Research (IPR), Gandhinagar; and Centre for Environment Education (CEE), Ahmedabad.

He has had quite a few of his research works published with respected national/international journals. To add to the list, he has also had an edited book published with IGI Global, USA, entitled *Progressive Trends in Electronic Resource Management in Libraries*.

As a resource person, Dr. Nihar K. Patra has visited different universities and institutions to deliver lectures on ERM and other technological advances in libraries. His area of interest in terms of research is on ERM, and digital libraries.

FOREWORD

Thirteen years ago I stepped into the academic library profession during a time of tremendous change. The world was going digital. Many people in higher education had fully adapted to using computers and the Internet to get a lot of their information. Our library users' needs, expectations, and demands were changing rapidly. At the same time, libraries still had majority print collections but we could see the onslaught of electronic resources coming our way.

At this point, a new area of the field known as the Electronic Resources Librarians was popping up in many libraries to begin to manage this new material. Often these professionals were the only ones in their organization that understood all the complexities involved in negotiating, ordering, licensing, acquiring, providing access, troubleshooting, and evaluating. They often had to be the flexible, nimble, and creative in accomplishing their increasingly complex work.

In the first few years, librarians were expanding e-content collections (or holdings) and trying to use tools and methods they've used in the print world for acquiring and collecting. But it was clear that more tools, new methods, and common (or established) practices were necessary. As I looked around the profession, I didn't see a single place or meeting where librarians can talk through these methods and where system vendors and librarians could discuss their emerging needs.

In 2006, together with a group of dedicated librarians, I hosted the first Electronic Resources & Libraries (ER&L) Conference. The first year involved a lot of finding our colleagues who do similar work in this new niche area of libraries. We learned a lot from each other about best practices and best ways to work with colleagues, other library departments, and users. Also, working with electronic content was impacting more librarians than just Electronic Resources Librarians. I saw the need for library departments (including IT, reference, instruction, collection development, and cataloging) to come together to increase organizational communications. We made sure the ER&L Conference brought these perspectives as well.

I've hosted 10 ER&L conferences since that first one and there continues to be more and more to learn. There are new business models that bring content quickly and on-demand for users. There are electronic resource management systems and other tools meant to help libraries better manage all aspects of e-resource management. There are new assessment metrics and analysis to help ensure libraries have the right resources and are making the content discoverable and accessible. There are new conversations about open access electronic content and the unique challenges of handling e-books.

There's still a lot to learn about the best ways to manage electronic resources, the best ways to troubleshoot users' needs, and the most seamless ways to provide access to digital content. The profession needs library workers and leaders who have the mindset, tools, preparation, and skills to manage electronic content. Continued professional development through books, conferences, and online learning is essential for the modern librarian, especially those working in and around electronic resource management.

It is with this in mind that I write this foreword to Dr. Nihar K. Patra's book. Dr. Patra's many years of experience with digital libraries and electronic resource management are demonstrated in this publication. He communicates the many aspects of managing electronic resources as well as providing a real-world case study to help the reader understand electronic resource collection development, electronic resource lifecycle management, and the needed IT infrastructure.

I encourage anyone who picked up this book to read it and learn from it. It will help a student or professional become familiar with the evolution of technology that has led to the proliferation of electronic resources, understand the many aspects of electronic resource management, evaluate electronic resource management systems, and learn best practices from the field.

B. Tijerina
Data & Society Research Institute, New York, NY,
United States

PREFACE

Taking a quick look at libraries in the past and now, it can be said that the paradigm shift that the introduction of advanced technological concepts and mechanisms brought in has pervaded and changed library users, professionals, and resource management, in the most dynamic way. My years of professional involvement in the field have provided me with the scope to trace the eventual dilution of cumbersome library practices, and their replacement with the more efficient and diverse e-resources management concept that I have discussed through my studies and in the chapters of my book *Digital Disruption and Electronic Resource Management in Libraries.*

The vast body of e-resources that has been made available to users, as well as aspirants for librarianship courses, needs to be discussed in an in-depth manner, to not only understand the avenues of research and information gathering that they present, but also to understand the future scope of libraries. The study also answers the question of how e-resources should be managed so that users can access material effectively and efficiently. Researchers in this field would surely understand that even though the electronic medium is a brilliantly efficient one, and has the potential to reach out to millions of people within seconds, there are loopholes and drawbacks. Moreover, in most cases, institutions that are inclined to digitally improve their system of spreading information do not consider the cost of maintenance that ensues with the change in format. However, there is no denying the fact that with the changing facets of the industry, an awareness looms that libraries need to upgrade their scale of operations.

To fit into the scheme of things, librarians, both experienced and beginners, are facing the need to acquire technical knowledge about e-resources and their management. Since libraries are primarily visited by students, research scholars, professors, and faculty members of institutions, it is the duty of the authorities to present them with unadulterated information from the best available sources in the shortest amount of time, and provide them with access in a most scientific way. The need for an integrated system comes with more attention to the collection, authentication, selection, and availability of the resources. But, even though efforts have been made, smooth working with users and library infrastructure having a codependent relationship has been hindered. The policies and procedures implemented by organizations have resulted in slowing down the process of easy availability, and therefore they need the support of technically equipped staff who have an in-depth understanding of the scenario, as well as updated information about the technological advances in the field. I hope I have been able to guide my readers through the various ways in which electronic resource management has taken on traditional library formats.

The introductory chapter of my book would garner the attention of librarians who are currently struggling to understand the concept of e-resources management. Thankfully, the DLF had defined a specific standard for the development of ERM, which has been approved by renowned practitioners in the field, namely Jewell, Aipperspach, Anderson, England, Kasprowski, McQuillan, and several others. Moreover, the importance of e-resources in higher education has been discussed. Further researches in the field have determined that the conventional ILMS is not efficient enough to cater to the management of e-resource. Hence, ERMS with its list of benefits should be considered as a serious future undertaking that libraries in India have not yet adopted.

For those libraries who have already taken the plunge and are willing to explore newer avenues for electronic resource management, Chapter 2, From Electronic Resources to Electronic Resource Management, covers all the relevant areas. The success of the concept on intranet as well as on internet platforms has made it simpler for library users to not only access information, but also to store it for future reference, provided that they are granted the authority to do so. Codified for the purpose of computer information, these e-resources are digital files themselves, and are as important as the very system that creates and runs them. The varied types of electronic resources have also been discussed in the chapter. But, as well as how the concept of e-resource management has evolved, what deserves consideration are the two aspects of managing e-resources namely the front-end and back-end functions.

In Chapter 3, titled "Lifecycle of Electronic Resource Management," five major components of e-resource management are discussed. It is interesting to read the various components as it includes a list of directives to librarians or e-resource managers so that they can categorize the needs as well as care about the ergonomics of the digital infrastructure that is present within a library. As a librarian, it is not only essential to keep a note of the books and information that a library should contain and upgrade for the better guidance and support of users, it is also necessary to understand the budget of the organization and digitally enhance the e-resource mechanism that runs it, without going overboard. Also, the decision to select the best e-resources should be taken after proper consultation with experts, and should be considered after proper examination using different criteria/methods. This itself opens up professional opportunities for technically trained people who can assist librarians to ensure the complete security of information, as well as authentication and ease of availability.

Even though practicing librarians can get an idea of the best open source resources, as well as commercially viable ERMS (Electronic Resource Management Systems) that are in use today, it is not easy to sort out the best ones that would ensure complete operational safety for an organization. The comparison table in Chapter 4, An Electronic Resource Management and its Best Practice, discussed the comparison of 10 ERMS on functionality, standards, features and modules.

"Standards, Compatibility and Best Practices for Electronic Resource Management" elaborates on the various compatibilities and standards that have been adopted for ERMS. Reduction in administrative costs in libraries should be one of the main concerns, besides improvement of standards for e-resource management. Thus, reinforcing ERMS along with ILMS has been proven to be the best way to conduct electronic resource management efficiently.

In the chapter titled "Electronic Resource Management Systems: Pros and Cons," we have everything that a librarian needs to known to work with e-resources. Among the major concerns that crop up while dealing with such sensitive issues are licensing and agreements. The product might just be great and the perfect addition to your library for its renewable appeal, but if you have not reviewed the licensing agreements well before zeroing in on it, you might end up with major legal troubles later on. Mentioning the rights of users, composers, and library staff over a product is very necessary, as this will ensure that in future only authorized users can gain access to the product. In fact, copyright registration aspects have also been discussed which would lessen duplication of content and protect the rights of writers and contributors to a library, thereby giving a positive impression. What is brought to light is the fact that library staff can no longer choose to keep themselves limited within the sphere of physical books, journals, and periodicals if they wish to offer holistic assistance to members and users of their organization.

An elaborate case study sums up the final chapter on "Implementation of Electronic Resource Management in Libraries: A Case Study." Since the main concern resonating throughout the book is the management of e-resources in libraries, the study focuses on the implementation of ERM in libraries of management institutes in India, as well as on the loopholes in the practices and policies that govern the management of these resources. Readers also get an idea of how factors affecting the better management of e-resources lead to the optimal use of resources, and how libraries in management institutes are addressing various issues for maximum positive outcomes.

Studying through comparison is the best way to improve. Though India is fast catching up with management principles of e-resource and library resource upgrading policies, we are not the initiators. Several libraries around the world have already implemented ERMS, including institutes like the MIT, Cambridge University, Stanford University, University of Texas, and several others. Studies done by academic researchers there have been taken as a starting point and a well-defined format for my study and, therefore, these preexisting models have served as my guidance for elaborating on certain points in my study. The big picture of ERM becomes clear from the examples and authentic references, which will serve as a guide for many pursuing librarians, as they have for me.

The compact research work that has been put together in every chapter makes it easy to differentiate between the existence of information and the formation of knowledge. As I have myself learned a lot while trying to record the research work in print, I believe it will be an enriching experience for all readers.

ACKNOWLEDGMENTS

It is wonderful to note that this book attempts to almost entirely stand on the shoulders of the Library Information Science Community, especially those that deal with e-resources. As an extended version of my PhD thesis awarded by the Sambalpur University, India. In the year 2015, this book takes its cue from it. I am greatly thankful to my professional friends for suggesting to me to take ahead the thesis and give it the form of a book. I would like to thank and extend my gratitude to my revered teachers and supervisors, Prof. B.K. Choudhury and Prof. A.K. Pani, XLRI, for their constant and inspiring guidance, encouragement, support, affection, and patience that enabled me to carry out the research work. It is their blessings, constant encouragement, untiring, and endless effort, which helped me shape the thesis into the present form of a book.

I am also thankful to my friends and professional colleagues Akhtar Hussain and Late Bharat Kumar, who have ardently supported me throughout the duration of the project.

I greatly appreciate the publishing opportunity and efforts provided by the team at Elsevier Publishing. I specially want to thank George Knott and Lindsay C. Lawrence for their invaluable assistance, guidance, and patience through all the stages of project completion.

I would forever be indebted to my parents Sh. Nanda Kishore Patra and Smt. Saraswati Patra, who have always been a fountainhead of motivation and inspiration for me. Their constant support enabled me to pursue higher education, and encouraged me to carry out this project with dedication. The moral support and encouragement that have been extended by my family members, particularly my brothers Tarun Kumar Patra and Rashmi Ranjan Patra, sisters-in-law Tanuja Patra and Smrutimayee Patra, and nephews Tatwadarshi Patra and Divyesh Patra is indeed invaluable and unforgettable.

LIST OF ABBREVIATIONS

AIMS	Acharya Institute of Management and Sciences
API	Application Programming Interface
ASER	Access System for Electronic Resources
BI	*Business India*
BT	*Business Today*
BW	*Business World*
CD-ROM	Compact Disc Read-Only
COinS	Context Objects in Spans
CORAL	Centralized Online Resource Acquisition and Licensing
CORE	Cost of Resource Exchange
COUNTER	Counting Online Usage of Networked Electronic Resources
DLF—ERMI	Digital Library Federation—Electronic Resource Management Initiative
DLF	Digital Library Foundation
DOI	Digital Object Identifier
DRM	Digital Right Management
ER	Electronic Resources
E-RESOURCES	Electronic Resources
ERLIC	Electronic Resource Licensing Information Centre
ERM	Electronic Resource Management
ERMI	Electronic Resource Management Initiative
ERMS	Electronic Resource Management System
FMS	Faculty of Management Studies
FRBR	Functional Requirement for Bibliographic Records
GLIM	Great Lakes Institute of Management
HERMIES	Hopkins Electronic Resource Management System
HERMIS	Electronic Resource Management and Information Solutions
I²	Institutional Identifier
IAMT	Integrated Academy of Management and Technology
IBS	ICFAI Business School
IFMR	Institute for Financial Management and Research
IIFM	Indian Institute of Forest Management
IIFT	Indian Institute of Foreign Trade
IIM	Indian Institute of Management
ILL	Inter Library Loan
ILMS	Integrated Library Management System
ILS	Integrated Library Systems
IMI	International Management Institute
IMS	Institute of Management Studies
IMT	Institute for Management and Technology
IOTA	Improving OpenURLs Through Analytics
IP	Internet Protocol
IPE	Institute of Public Enterprise
IR	Institutional Repository

IRM	Institute of Rural Management
ISB	Indian School of Business
ISBD (ER)	International Standard Bibliographic Description for Electronic Resources
ISBN	International Standard Book Number
ISM	International School of Management
ISNI	International Standard for Name Identifier
ISTC	International Standard Text Code
IT	Information Technology
JBIMS	Jamanalal Baja Institute of Management Studies
KBART	Knowledge Bases and Related Tools
KJSIMSR	K J Somaiya Institute of Management Studies and Research
LAMP	Linux, Apache, MySQL, Perl
LBSIM	Lal Bahadur Shastri Institute of Management
LDAP	Lightweight Directory Access Protocol
LEWG	License Expression Working Group
LIBA	Loyola Institute of Business Administration
MARC	Machine Readable Catalogue
MDI	Management Development Institute
METS	Metadata Encoding and Transmission Standard
MODS	Metadata Object Description Schema
MPEG	Moving Picture Experts Group
NIM	NIRMA Institute of Management
NISO	National Information Standards Organization
NITIE	National institute of Industrial Engineering
OCLC	Online Computer Library Center
OLT	ONIX for Licensing Terms
ONIX	Online Information eXchange for Serials
OPAC	Online Public Access Catalog
PIE-J	Presentation and Identification of E-Journals
PSGIM	PSG Institute of Management
RCM	Regional College of Management
RSO	Reduced Sign On
RSS	Rich Site Summary/Really Simple Syndication
SERU	Shared Electronic Resource Understanding
SGML	Standardized General Markup Language
SIMS	Symbiosis Institute of Management Studies
SOAP	Simple Object Access Protocol
SOH	ONIX for Serials Online Holdings
SPJIMR	S P Jain Institute of Management Research
SRN	Serial Release Notification
SSO	Single Sign On System
SUSHI	Standardized Usage Harvesting Initiative
TAPMI	T A Pai Management Institute
TCP	Transmission Control Protocol
UBSPU	University Business School, Punjab University
URI	Uniform Resource Identifier
URL	Uniform Resource Locator

vCard	Electronic Business Card/Versit Card
VERA	Virtual Electronic Resource Access System
VGSM	Vinod Gupta School of Management
VPN	Virtual Private Network
VR	Virtual Reference
W3C	World Wide Web Consortium
WEDB	Web-based Database
WIMDR	Welingkar Institute of Management Development and Research
WSRP	Web Services for Remote Portlets
XIM	Xavier Institute of Management
XLRI	Xavier Labour Relation Institute
XML	Extendable Markup Language
XUL	XML User-interface Language

CHAPTER 1

Introduction

1.1 INTRODUCTION

Rather than stating that the world is changing, it would be more appropriate to state that the world has reached a state of holistic change, the reason being digital disruption. Digital disruption refers to advances in digital technologies that occur at a pace and magnitude that disrupt established ways of creating value, either within or across markets, social interactions, and more generally, our understanding and thinking. Digital disruption is essentially an opportunity, although it is often seen as a threat. Digital disruption occurs on many levels, such as in people's personal lives (e.g., mobile connectivity disrupts established work–life boundaries), work practices (e.g., new ways of communicating via social media changes the ways in which work is self-organized), business practices (e.g., workplace social media disrupts the way information travels in the organization and induces shifts in power relationships), industry structures (e.g., new digital intermediaries exploit information asymmetries in ways that reshape traditional value chains), societal (e.g., social media participation disrupts traditional practices of public opinion making, journalism, and politics) [1].

Libraries cannot be exempted from any changes that are affecting society, alongside other technological changes that are pervading the globe. The library world has also been hugely impacted by the disruptive technology phenomenon. The arrival and enormous growth rate of digital contents have fundamentally changed the way in which content is made available to library users. In recent years, libraries have been acquiring more and more electronic resources (e-resources) because of perceived benefits, such as easy access to information, and its comprehensiveness. Due to the influx of e-resources in libraries, the collection, acquisition, and maintenance of these resources have become complicated issues to deal with. This has forced libraries to devise strategies to manage and deliver e-resources conveniently. Therefore, "Management of E-resources" or "Electronic Resource Management" (ERM) has become

Digital Disruption and Electronic Resource Management in Libraries.
DOI: http://dx.doi.org/10.1016/B978-0-08-102045-6.00001-7

a challenge for library professionals that needs to be addressed through research and practice. To meet these challenges, library professionals and content providers have decided to develop an "Electronic Resource Management System" (ERMS) for management of e-resources in a more systematic way. Breeding [2] defined two aspects of managing e-resources. They include: (1) the front-end details of delivering the content to library users, and (2) managing the business details of back-end staff functions related to acquisition, payment, and licensing.

Being on the verge of transition from an old method to a new method, libraries are in need of clarity on different aspects of e-resource management. In order to bring clarity and acceptability, there is a need for research and innovation into different aspects of ERM. The adoption of ERM will lead to systematic management and optimal use of library resources. With this background, it is assumed that there should be no differences in the adoption and practice of e-resource management across libraries in business schools/institutes in India, which is discussed in Chapter 7, Implementation of Electronic Resource Management in Libraries: A Case Study. This homogeneity is assumed because of two reasons: (1) competitiveness, and (2) capacity to adopt new ideas.

1.2 BACKGROUND

The use of the latest form of e-resources in libraries began with the development of the machine-readable catalogue (MARC) format in the 1960s. E-resources have been increasingly accepted in Indian libraries and other libraries around the world since then. Their usage has been increased due to the accessibility, portability, and storage capacity of MARC. The last decade has witnessed a phenomenal increase in the use of e-resources such as e-journals, e-books, full-text/aggregated databases, digitized and born-digital documents, digital images, streaming video, sound, audio books, and internet/web resources in Indian libraries, because of their merits over print resources. As a result, e-resources have a significant impact on libraries and their users in both operational and organizational aspects today, besides bringing changes in library usage pattern and budgets. The increasing acquisition of paid e-resources providing seamless online access to users have posed major challenges, which include changes in a library's workflow such as selection, acquisition, copyright, license agreements, negotiation, cataloguing, and development of access interfaces, etc. The management aspect of e-resources mainly cover five areas such as: (1) collection development policies, (2) work-flow/lifecycle, (3) license agreements, (4) usage statistics, and (5) an e-resource librarian. In this context [3−6] opined that a library collection includes licensed as well as open access information resources. They suggested that the maintenance of a strong library policy ensures decision-making is consistent and the collective development of e-resources is more efficient and thorough. They also put forth the idea of formulation of an e-resources collection development policy that would ensure consistency in approach, appropriateness of e-resources requirement, and assessment of economic feasibility. The entire process of management of e-resources is known as lifecycle/workflow/discovery. Following this line [7−10], discussed that the concept of the lifecycle of ERM begins from selection, trial, evaluation, license agreement, acquisition, and access system, to troubleshooting. They have also addressed the major steps, processes, procedures, and issues involved in the lifecycle of e-resources that can serve as teaching tools for librarians. On the other hand, one of the important components in the lifecycle of e-resources is the reviewing of license agreements. In this context [6,11−14], listed some important deal-breaking factors while reviewing license agreements. These are access concern, i.e., authorized site, authorized users, breach cure period, confidentiality of business terms, dispute resolution and governing law, electronic reserves and course packs, indemnification, interlibrary lending and scholarly sharing, licensee's responsibility for action of authorized users, modification of license terms, perpetual use/archival rights, remote access, usage statistics, and many more. Another essential component of the lifecycle of e-resources is the usage report of e-resources. In this context [15,16], discussed that usage statistics are valuable tools that can be used to assess the frequency of usage of e-resources, which in turn can help during the time of renewal/cancelation of e-resources. Apart from the e-resources that are available on a paid basis, there are also some others that are available freely through open access content providers which have a positive impact on the organization's research work. However, a librarian needs to identify additional open access materials that systematically include those resources that are present within the scope of the institutional curriculum. They must be integrated within a local discovery service, so that there is a significant enhancement in e-resource collection which can be offered to users.

It has been observed that publication of books and journals have largely moved out of the print world, and have taken the electronic publication route. The question remains that, in the case of e-books, how do they fit within workflows and automation systems that were initially designed for print? New models of acquisition have emerged which pushed the customary strategies to the back foot, and have made resources available "just-in-time," rather than anticipating interest through the traditional "just-in-case" selection and acquisition process. Thus the patron driven acquisitions concept has been currently considered a model for selection and purchase of e-resources. It has gathered significant interest among librarians, as it offers benefits to users in the form of seamless and immediate access to e-collections. Another factor, such as Cost–benefit analysis, should also be considered when libraries begin to invest in e-resources which can help in strengthening the value of its subscriptions.

In addition to the above, there is a further factor that deserves immediate attention. It is about devising efficient ways to ensure the optimal access to users (students and faculty members) of resources before library professionals. To address this issue, methods, norms, and standards are being developed for the management of e-resources in libraries through continuous research and innovation. The Digital Library Federation—Electronic Resource Management Initiative (DLF − ERMI) took the initiatives in research and innovation which led to the development of common specifications, standards, and tools for managing license agreements, related administrative information, and internal processes associated with collections of licensed e-resources [17]. Implementation of standards is indispensable for the development of ERM. The report produced by the ERMI in August 2004, which was sponsored by the DLF, has become the de facto standard for development of ERM. In the context of standards used for ERM [18−20], have described the best practice ERM standards as being divided into five categories such as: (1) link resolvers and knowledge bases which include OpenURL, KBART, and IOTA; (2) the work, its manifestations and access points covers DOI, MARC21, ONIX for Serials, ONIX for books, PIE-J, and TRANSFER; (3) integration of usage and cost-related data includes CORE, COUNTER, and SUSHI; (4) coding license terms and defining consensus includes OLT and SERU; and finally, (5) data exchange using institutional identifiers includes I^2, WorldCat Registry, Shibboleth, and vCard. Similarly [21], discussed two important standards to provide usage statistics, which are COUNTER and SUSHI.

Due to the influx of e-resources coupled with recent technological innovations like Google search, Google scholar, amazon.com, etc., library users often compare these services and their e-resources with services offered by libraries, and expect similar simple and convenient access to e-resources from libraries. As a corollary, these developments make it a challenging job for librarians to manage the collection and development of e-resources. Many librarians found the management of e-resources difficult and cumbersome, because existing integrated library management systems are not capable enough of supporting the management of e-resources. The development of ERMS, either through in-house expertise or a commercial/proprietary product, is a ground-breaking innovation in the line of library management that has the right resources to be adequate. ERMS is basically a tool for libraries, and it directly caters to the needs of end-users. It is a one-stop solution for managing and accessing e-resources which develop with specific standards and compatibility. Refs. [22−24] have explained that the main purpose of ERMS is to manage the workflow of e-resources, to access and centralize data, and to improve administrative interfaces, etc. They have discussed different software available in the market, both from commercial and open sources. Some of these ERMS include Innovative Interface's Innovative ERM, TDNet's TDNet ERM Solutions, Ex Libris's Verde ERM, OCLC's Web-Share License Manager, SemperTool's SMDB, University of Notre Dame's CORAL, MIT's VERA, Serials Solutions' 360 Resource Manager, HARRASSOWITZ's HERMIS, The Johns Hopkins University's HERMIES, Colorado Alliance's Gold Rush, WT Cox's Journal Finder, EBSCO's EBSCONET ERM Essentials, Simon Fraser University Library's CUFTS, SIRSI Corp's E-Resource Center, and Priory Solution's Research Monitor. There are also different tools available today that can help users easily access e-resources by different authors. Refs. [19,25−27] discussed that e-resources can be given access through online public access catalogues (OPACs), A-to-Z lists, subject indexes, link resolvers, one-stop search through federated or discovery search engines, browsing lists such as database lists, embedded lists such as links to web pages, and remote access such as Shibboleth, EZproxy, and Athens.

It has been observed that the involvement of e-resources has reshaped all aspects of organization and management strategies in libraries. "Acquisition librarians" evaluate, negotiate, and acquire the collections; "reference librarians" provide end-user support; "technical librarians" or "web librarians" develop or implement tools that provide remote access to users; "subject specialists" and "collection development teams" take decisions on the new resources that need to be acquired and the ones that need to be canceled/renewed in any given year. The collection development team is assigned to maintain a proper balance between print and e-resources. Therefore, library staff are responsible for managing all aspects of e-resources, and should always include a dedicated professional for managing e-resources. Refs. [28−30] opined that an e-resource librarian needs to be recruited, and they should be skillful communicators and collaborators, have good experience in technology, and be well-versed in issues related to e-resources, such as licensing, troubleshooting access problems, cataloguing, record management for non-OPAC systems, site monitoring for content and access changes, and setting up links for full-text, etc.

1.3 ROLE OF E-RESOURCES IN HIGHER EDUCATION

E-resources play an important role in the scenario of higher education. "Library," "resources," and "education" are three indissoluble and indivisible concepts. These three are not only vitally and concomitantly related to each other, they are in fact coexistent. Currently, libraries provide a "one-stop solution" for print and e-resources, including titles from commercially aggregated databases and free titles. The easy of availability of e-resources have led to an increase in the demand for research and academic materials. They have become more popular because of the set of incredible benefits that they bring to organizations, students, faculties, and research scholars. A few benefits have been discussed below, but they are not limited to just the ones mentioned:

1. Simultaneous searching and accessibility by multiple users.
2. Searching by keywords help the academician and researchers in building an environment where work-isolation has become irrelevant [31].
3. Searches can be conducted through various search engines.
4. Before acquisition e-books, e-journals, abstracts of the journals, or content of the books can be accessed and reviewed by faculties, research scholars, and students. Based on their recommendations, these can be purchased for the library.
5. The users appreciate the ways of online searching, browsing, scanning, retrieval, and even submission of manuscripts, as it saves their time and increases work productivity [32].
6. Knowledge sharing can be done through transfer of electronic files via e-mail, messengers, and other media.

7. Research publications in online journals help accomplish and enhance the level of research output. Consequently, they increase the professional visibility of the institute.

Considering these benefits, students and research scholars in most universities/institutions access e-resources to support their academic and research work.

The majority of institutions/universities have e-resources such as e-journals, e-books, and e-databases of companies and industries which face constant demands from a huge body of users. Keeping in mind the changing demands of the users, many institutes/universities form a consortium of e-resources, mainly e-journals, to offer advantages like: (1) reduction in subscription costs, (2) coverage of e-resources is high with optimum utilization of funds, (3) cost-sharing for technical and training support, (4) facilities to build digital library networks, (5) negotiation of better terms of license agreements for e-resources, etc. The e-resources that are highly demanded in libraries include e-journals, e-books, and "country, company, and industry databases." With these e-resources in hand, libraries not only find it easier to increase the usage of library services, but it also enables the growth of the institute's research, publications, and learning.

1.4 ROLE OF THE ELECTRONIC RESOURCE MANAGER

With the increase in involvement with the collection of e-resources in a library, it is important for the library staff to manage job functions including planning, selection, evaluation, implementation, access, and renewal/cancelation. Just in the way that the job responsibilities of each of acquisition librarian, systems librarian, serial librarian, and reference librarian in a print section is different, in a similar way of the role of an e-resource librarian or e-resource manager is also distinct and well-defined. The job responsibility of an e-resource librarian differs from library-to-library. However, it should be noted that strong technical and interpersonal skills are common qualities that all e-resource librarians must exhibit. Engel and Robbins [29] discussed how the specific job titles, job responsibilities, and job qualifications vary by institution. A holistic study of the evolution of the e-resource librarian, and the role they currently play within academic libraries, can provide guidance to administrators seeking to create similar positions within their own institutions. Such a study can also help library and information studies educators develop the curriculum, as well as educate graduate students interested in pursuing similar positions upon completion of a course.

The library professional within the organization develops the expertise and knowledge to manage e-resources. The common job responsibilities of an e-resource manager are as follows, but are not limited to:

1. Initiating new e-resource acquisitions following procedures like selection, evaluation, negotiation of license agreements, etc.
2. Negotiation with vendors and publishers.
3. Organizing e-resources in a timely manner in a variety of systems enables access to e-resources by users such as the ERMS, link resolver, A-to-Z database list, discovery tool, and library portals.
4. Managing and maintaining troubleshooting problems arising from the acquisition of e-resources, licensing, or access-related technical issues, including ERMS, link resolution, federated searching, discovery tool, and library portals.
5. Maintaining teamwork and collaboration with staff, administrators, librarians, publishers, and vendors.
6. Establishing policies and procedures that coordinate acquisitions and create metadata with national standards, local policy, and procedures.
7. Evaluation of a vendor's performance and monitoring of their services, and compiling usage statistics of e-resources which helps in the renewal/cancelation of e-resource for the next financial year.

To support students, faculties, and staff, and to promote excellence in global society, an e-resources librarian should have a background rich in diverse experiences, along with management of teamwork and cooperatives, alongside having a techno-savvy perspective into work activities, thereby establishing the e-resource system as a single point of access for authorized users from any devices that access the web.

1.5 PARITY OF ELECTRONIC RESOURCE MANAGEMENT IN LIBRARY MANAGEMENT

There can be no amount of comparison between traditional resources and e-resources, as they are completely different from each other with regard to functions, features, and sizes; however, the workflow/lifecycle process of both resources have some similarities. Here, the overall management of e-resources become much more similar with that of a typical library management. In general, the tasks that fall within the scope of library management include acquisition (planning, budget, selection, purchase, payment, and renewal/cancelation in the case of periodical subscriptions), processing of acquisition materials (accession, classification, and cataloguing), and ensuring availability of resources to the users (OPAC, patron check in/out materials, and interlibrary loans). Similarly, in the case of e-resource management, it includes acquisition (budget, selection, trial, evaluation, negotiation of license agreements, payment, and renewal/cancelation), processing of acquired e-resources (integration with different tools such as ERMS, link resolver, A-to-Z database list, discovery tool, and library portal), and making them available to users (authorized users can download, copy, and send e-mail through e-resources and interlending facilities). So, the tasks that are a part of the ongoing process in a library find their purpose in e-resource management as well, only in a more technically adept way.

1.6 EMERGING THOUGHTS ON THE NEW DYNAMICS OF ELECTRONIC RESOURCE MANAGEMENT

In recent years, libraries have become increasingly involved with electronic materials and the collection of digital objects, in addition to the traditional print inventory. The original model of integrated library systems was designed primarily for print materials, and therefore lacked the functionality needed for managing subscriptions for e-resources. As e-resources grew into a dominant academic library collection, a new genre of software called the ERMS emerged. These products were designed to manage all the business processes involved in licensing of e-resources, and to describe the contents of each package or portfolio to which the library subscribed. The idea of managing e-resources on a separate platform than that of print has not yet met with major success. The genre of ERMSs has not thrived, despite the overwhelming need that libraries have in this area.

The current phase of library automation has seen the emergence of new systems, called library services platforms, that take a more comprehensive approach to managing library collections. These systems come with the ability to manage all types of library resources, including print, electronic, and digital materials, with support for the metadata formats and business models needed to acquire and describe all formats. Rather than managing e-resources as a separate activity, these products support the business rules associated with managing subscriptions and other specialized requirements, while still taking advantage of workflow tools, functionality, metadata, and knowledge bases that apply to all aspects of the collection. So much of the business processes were involved in managing e-resources that they overlapped with that of the print collection which included vendor records, accounting files, and invoices, as well as bibliographic metadata. Thus the concept of a separate ERMS resulted in significant duplication of effort and redundancy of data. The ever-changing nature of library collections, where the proportions of e-resources is most likely to increase even further, that what print materials would have for a long term. To combat the situation, the model of comprehensive resource management holds greater promise than the notion of separate applications dedicated to each format of material.

REFERENCES

[1] K. Riemer, U. Gal, J. Hamann, B. Gilchriest, M. Teixeira, Digital disruptive intermediaries: finding new digital opportunities by disrupting existing business models, 2015. Retrieved September 14, 2016, from http://hdl.handle.net/2123/12761.

[2] M. Breeding, The many facets of managing electronic resources, Comput. Libraries Westport 24 (1) (2004) 25−33.

[3] K. Kempf, Collection development in the digital age, JLIS 4 (2) (2013) 267−273. Retrieved September 19, 2015, from http://leo.cilea.it/index.php/jlis/article/viewFile/8857/8029.

[4] S. Corrall, The concept of collection development in the digital world, in: M. Fieldhouse, A. Marshall (Eds.), Collection Development in the Digital Age, Facet, London, 2012, pp. 3−25.

[5] S. Mangrum, M.E. Pozzebon, Use of collection development policies in electronic resource management, Collection Building 31 (3) (2012) 108−114.

[6] S. Johnson, O.G. Evensen, J. Gelfand, G. Lammers, L. Sipe, N. Zilper, Key issues for e-resource collection development: a guide for libraries. IFLA, 3−32, 2012. Retrieved September 19, 2015, from http://www.ifla.org/files/assets/acquisition-collection-development/publications/Electronic-resource-guide.pdf.

[7] R.O. Weir, Learning the basics of electronic resource management, in: R.O. Weir (Ed.), Managing Electronic Resources: A LITA Guide, ALA Techsource, Chicago, 2012, pp. 1−16.

[8] S. Joshipura, Selecting, acquiring, and renewing electronic resources, in: H. Yu, S. Breivold (Eds.), Electronic Resource Management in Libraries: Research and Practice, Information Science Publishing, Hershey, 2008, pp. 46−65.

[9] J. Poe, M. Bevis, J.B. Graham, B. Latham, K.W. Stevens, Sharing the albatross of e-resources management workflow, in: H. Yu, S. Breivold (Eds.), Electronic Resource Management in Libraries: Research and Practice, Information Science Publishing, Hershey, 2008, pp. 71−89. Retrieved September 19, 2015, from http://xa.yimg.com/kq/groups/2584474/2140640795/name/Electronic_Resource_Management_in_Libraries__Research_and_Practice__Premier_Referene_Source_.pdf.

[10] M. Breeding, Helping you buy: electronic resource management systems, Comput. Libraries 28 (7) (2008), Retrieved April 1, 2014, from http://www.librarytechnology.org/ltg-displaytext.pl?RC=13437.

[11] J. Emery, G. Stone, TERMS: techniques for electronic resource management, Library Technol. Rep. 49 (2) (2013) 5−43. Retrieved September 19, 2015 from http://eprints.hud.ac.uk/16113.

[12] T.L. Davis, C. Feather, The evolution of license content, in: H. Yu, S. Breivold (Eds.), Electronic Resource Management in Libraries: Research and Practice, Information Science Publishing, Hershey, 2008, pp. 122−144.

[13] K.C. Brown, Tactics and terms in the negotiation of electronic resource licenses, in: H. Yu, S. Breivold (Eds.), Electronic Resource Management in Libraries: Research and Practice, Information Science Publishing, Hershey, 2008, pp. 174−192.

[14] B. Albitz, Licensing and Managing Electronic Resources, Chandos Publishing, Oxford, 2008.

[15] K. Wikoff, Electronics Resources Management in the Academic Library: A Professional Guide, Libraries Unlimited, Santa Barbara, CA, 2012.

[16] P. Hults, Electronic usage statistics, in: H. Yu, S. Breivold (Eds.), Electronic Resource Management in Libraries: Research and Practice, Information Science Publishing, Hershey, 2008, pp. 29−46.

[17] DLF, 2004. Retrieved December 3, 2014, from http://old.diglib.org/standards/dlf-erm02.htm.

[18] T. Jewell, J. Aipperspach, I. Anderson, D. England, R. Kasprowski, B. McQuillan, et al., Making Good on the Promise of ERM: A Standards and Best Practices Discussion Paper, NISO, Baltimore, 2012.

[19] A.C. Elguindi, K. Schmidt, Electronic Resource Management: Practical Perspectives in a New Technical Services Model, Chandos, Oxford, 2012.

[20] R. Kasprowski, Standards in electronic resource management, Bull. Am. Soc. Inf. Sci. Technol. 33 (6) (2007) 32−37.

[21] D.E. Williams, K.A. Plummer, F.J. Bove, Tech services on the web, Tech. Serv. Q. 25 (4) (2008) 95−102.

[22] N.K. Patra, S. Jha, Comparative analysis of electronic resource management systems (ERMS): a web study, in: N.K. Patra, B. Kumar, A.K. Pani (Eds.), Progressive Trends in Electronic Resource Management in Libraries, Information Science Publishing, Hershey, 2014, pp. 118−146.

[23] K.J.P. Anbu, S. Kataria, S. Ram, Dynamics of managing electronic resources: electronic resource management system (ERMS) initiatives, DESIDOC J. Library Inf. Technol. 33 (4) (2013) 300−305.

[24] C.A. Ruttenberg, Finding the tool that fits best: cloud based task management for electronic resources, OCLC Sys. Serv. 29 (3) (2013) 151−160.

[25] P. Babbar, Towards innovative library services: a case study of Indra Gandhi National Open University, India, in: N.K. Patra, B. Kumar, A.K. Pani (Eds.), Progressive Trends in Electronic Resource Management in Libraries, Information Science Publishing, Hershey, 2014, pp. 221−235.

[26] G. Stachokas, Managing electronic resources accessible, in: Ryan O. Weir (Ed.), Managing Electronic Resources: A LITA Guide, ALA TechSource, Chicago, 2012, pp. 69−85.

[27] M.G. Sreekumar, Strategies on e-resources management for smart information systems, Ann. Library Inf. Stud. (ALIS) 59 (3) (2012) 155−169.

[28] D. Murdock, Relevance of electronic resource management systems to hiring practices of electronic resources personnel, Library Collections, Acquisitions, Tech. Serv. 34 (1) (2010) 25−42.

[29] D. Engel, S. Robbins, Evolving roles for electronic resources librarians, in: H. Yu, S. Breivold (Eds.), Electronic Resource Management in Libraries: Research and Practice, Information Science Publishing, Hershey, 2008, pp. 105−120.

[30] E.F. Duranceau, C. Hepfer, Staffing for electronic resource management: the results of a survey, Serials Rev. 28 (4) (2002) 316–320.

[31] R.K. Sharma, E-resource availability and importance for higher education and research in India, Learn. Comm. 1 (2011) 35–42.

[32] P.P. Rani, J. Geetha, Electronic resources in the modern libraries: a new path. Paper presented at the 5th International CALIBER -2007, Punjab University, Chandigarh, 2007, February. Retrieved December 03, 2015 from http://ir.inflibnet.ac.in/bitstream/handle/1944/1444/696-701.pdf?sequence=1.

CHAPTER 2

From Electronic Resources to Electronic Resource Management

2.1 DEFINITION OF ELECTRONIC RESOURCES

The term e-resource has been defined in varied ways, using a number of different names. While some authorities use the term "digital resources," others refer to the "digital collection," which means the same thing.

E-resources, as defined by allwords.com, is information which can be stored in the form of electronic signals and made available to all, but not necessarily on a computer [1]. According to AACR2 2002 Revision: 2003 Update, an electronic resource is "Material (data and/or program(s)) encoded for manipulation by a computerized device. This material may require the use of a peripheral which is directly connected to a computerized device (e.g., CD-ROM drive), or perhaps a connection to a computer network (e.g., the internet)." This definition, however, excludes the e-resources which do not require the use of a computer. For example, compact discs and video discs containing music do not require a computer to complement its usability. An e-resource is an electronic information resource which can be accessed on the intranet, as well as on the internet. Users can get the required information whenever they want. "An e-resource is a collection of digital content delivery to the user via the internet" [2]. The International Standard Bibliographic Description for Electronic Resources (ISBD-ER) defined electronic resources as the materials which are codified for computer elaboration, including those materials that require the use of computer peripherals [3,4]. The International Records Management Trust defined an electronic record as any component of information that is produced through electronic ways, which means that they are both a part of an electronic resource that can be stored in digital files, as well as digital records themselves. Every electronic record consists of at least one digital object, component, or element, such as bits of data collected together to form a word processed document. Some electronic records, such as photographs, video clips, or web pages, may contain many different objects or elements.

Digital Disruption and Electronic Resource Management in Libraries.
DOI: http://dx.doi.org/10.1016/B978-0-08-102045-6.00002-9

The best way to structure and organize e-resources is by sorting them according to their format. Though it is possible to attempt different approaches, i.e., adopt a different distribution medium (CD-ROM, web, and internet sources), go by subject coverage, or through content arrangement (full-texts, citations, etc.), Armstrong and Lonsdale [5] discussed that JUSTEIS has suggested all resources are often viewed as variants on search engines. It is therefore necessary to distinguish databases from e-journals, and e-books from open access archives. Tara [6] discussed in his powerpoint presentation that there are three types of electronic resources:

1. Digital Communications: this includes social networking sites, online tutorials, e-mails, massage boards, blogs, and online classroom instruction sites;
2. Digital Collections: this includes online audio and video collections, websites, online image collections, online periodicals and book collections, online documents and wikis; and
3. Online Finding Aids: this includes indexes, search engines, and databases.

2.2 ELECTRONIC RESOURCES: A BIRD'S-EYE VIEW

With the advent of new-age technology, librarians have taken the leap and adopted computer/information technology to access library resources efficiently. In the mid-1960s the MARC (Machine Readable Cataloguing) format developed, and then the use of e-resources in libraries started. During the early 1970s, libraries provided access to data sets, and during the 1980s libraries started to get software and data on diskettes, and offered databases on CD-ROM which contained full-text with search interfaces, thereby introducing a microcomputer revolution. In 1990, Tim Berners-Lee created the World Wide Web (www). The creation of the www triggered the concept of online public library catalogues (OPAC). The subsequent development of the Mosaic browser in 1992 led to extensive use of the web, beginning in 1993. With the advent of web-based search engines like Google and Yahoo, e-resources became easily available. Eventually, libraries started offering bibliographic as well as full-text databases, e-books, and e-journals, along with web-based catalogues, to their users.

A range of e-resources became available to libraries from the 1960s to the early 2000s. They are discussed below.

2.2.1 Online Catalogue

In the mid-1960s, the Machine Readable Catalogue became the medium through which e-resources could access library resources. MARC was used for automation, and it supported the data standard in technology development. From the time of its inception, it ensured that library resources were accessed through the right processes.

2.2.2 Machine Readable Cataloguing

During the 1960s, the Library of Congress, USA, developed the MARC format. It is basically a standard digital format that helps in the creation, as well as exchange of, catalogues between libraries through bibliographic descriptions. MARC formats went on to become the national standard for dissemination of bibliographic data in 1971, and the international standard in 1973. The MARC1 was created, and codes were designed with the help of computer software to put together bibliographic elements, such as the name of the publisher and place of publication. The language and procedures were consequently developed and documented. The Library of Congress decided to work on the MARC2 format in March 1967 to serve as a medium of communication to exchange information. Thus, the development of the MARC format laid the foundation for libraries to share bibliographic data among themselves. MARC has several versions, and the most popular among them is MARC21. MARC21 was formed in 1999 as a result of the synchronization of the United States and Canadian MARC formats, and UNIMARC. MARC21 includes the format for bibliographic records, as well as the formats for classification schedules, authority records, and holdings records.

2.2.3 Shared Cataloguing

Frederick G. Kilgour [7] in 1967 established the Ohio College Library Center (OCLC), which was the world's first computerized library network. In 1971 OCLC created the shared cataloguing database which is now known as WorldCat. It supports 54 academic libraries in Ohio. With the help of this popular online cataloguing system, bibliographic records between libraries are shared well, thus saving expenses in developing their own library catalogues.

2.2.4 Online Public Access Catalogue

OPAC stands for Online Public Access Catalogue. Ohio State University Libraries, in 1975, installed computers to search the library catalogue through various access points such as title, author, call number, keyword, and Library of Congress subject headings. The online catalogues were developed to replace existing library card catalogues during the 1980s. These online catalogues improved the search potential and scope of users, but their utilities were not just limited to this. These systems were also integrated with circulation and acquisitions processing. This resulted in putting together additional information regarding the status of an order in process, and also about circulation updates [8]. OPACs of different library automation software are now available in the market as VTLS-Vertua, Libsys, Alice for Windows, SOUL, Koha, etc.

2.2.5 Web-Based Catalogues

Web-based catalogues defined the electronic representations of information about the products and/or services of an organization. Web-based catalogues were offered through graphical user interfaces with a Boolean search facility, which was "still a retrieval technique designed for trained and experienced users" [9].

2.2.6 Databases

A database is a system and setup where data is stored in an organized manner in a digital format, and is available to staff as well as library members for future reference purposes. Users can conduct searches on a database through authors, keywords, titles, and subjects with Boolean operators. Databases comprise of products such as directories, abstracts and indexes, encyclopedias, dictionaries, and other references works.

In the words of Moghaddam [10], a database is a "collection of data that is organized for easy storage and access. These include paper-based tools like dictionaries and libraries of print materials." Some databases are discussed below.

2.2.7 Bibliographic Databases

A bibliographic database contains bibliographic records. It is an organized collection of references to published digital literature, which includes conference proceedings, journals and newspaper articles, government and legal publications, patents, standards, reports, books, periodicals, etc. A large proportion of bibliographic data available in these databases generally belong to conference papers, articles, etc., rather than just monologues. These contain rich and relevant subject descriptions such as keywords, subject terms, and call numbers [11]. The first Dialog database software was created under Roger K. Summit's leadership at Lockheed in 1966 (Dialog was invented online in 1966). In the 1970s, computer-based bibliographic databases revolutionized bibliographic research. In 1972, Tymnet formed a commercial telecommunications network, which led database providers to offer services through the network [12]. During the 1980s, the use of library e-resources began to increase a lot.

2.2.8 CD-ROM Databases

CD-ROM stands for "Compact Disc Read-Only Memory." This is a type of optical disc having the capacity to store large amounts of data, up to 1GB. The most common storage capacity is 650MB. Databases stored on CD-ROM are defined as CD-ROM databases, where users can search for their queries using various features. Library Corporation's Biblio File produced the first commercial CD-ROM product which was mainly designed for libraries.

2.2.9 Online Databases

In the 1980s online databases were widely used. During the middle of the decade, full-text articles were added to online bibliographic databases. That was when databases started becoming more useful than ever. Online searches were made during this time, via the TELNET protocol and private for-profit networks. The internet was not used to conduct online searches at that time [13].

2.2.10 Web-Based Databases

Web-based databases (WBDBs) are basically structured lists of web pages [14]. According to Doe [15], WBDBs are collections of organized information which are used all the time. Wyllys [16] quoted in his powerpoint slides that Feiler [17] distinguished four main purposes for web-based databases such as, "publishing data on the web, sharing data on the web, e-commerce, and totally database-driven websites."

2.2.11 Electronic Journals

An electronic journal, also known as online journals, e-journals, and electronic serials, is basically complete text that is available in an electronic form. Electronic journals, accessed via electronic transmission, are usually published on the web.

Electronic journals first appeared during the 1970s, but they only gained popularity in 1996. Electronic journals, which are available in electronic media, such as floppy disc, CD-ROM, DVD, and online databases, can be accessed online. Electronic journals can be accessed through Gopher, FTP, Telnet, e-mail or discussion lists, but are mainly accessed through the web [18]. Generally, electronic journals are published in two different ways on the web, and they are commercial and open source. The main difference between the two types lies in one being a paid and purchased version (commercial), while the other is free to use (open source). Nowadays, most electronic journals are online publications, in contrast to some others which are digital versions of their already existing printed counterparts. The PDF is the most popular format used for electronic journals; however, some electronic journals are also published in HTML. Other formats that find mention in this list may include Doc., image, and MP3 audio. Electronic journals are available through an aggregator database, or directly through a publisher site such as EBSCOHOST, PROQUEST, Lexis-Nexis, JSTOR, Project Mouse, Science Direct, Emerald, etc.

2.2.12 Electronic Books

Electronic books are long for e-books. These are text- and image-based publications in digital format that can be read on computers or other digital devices. In 1971, an e-book was created as the first steps of Project Gutenberg; a domain digital library where users can access books from a public domain. "It is nearly 40 years old, already. But this is a short life compared to the five-century old print book" [19].

The Oxford Dictionary of English defines the e-book as "an electronic version of a printed book, but e-books can and do exist without any printed equivalent." Commercially produced e-books are read on dedicated e-book readers. For reading e-books, one can use mobile phones, computers, and smart phones, as well as other sophisticated electronic devices. Kindle versions available on Amazon are also popular ways of reading e-books. (Wikipedia, 16 July 2013). Borchers [20] defines an electronic book or e-book as "a portable hardware and software system that can display large quantities of readable textual information to the user, and that lets the user navigate through this information."

Most e-books can be read as PDF files, and hence reader applications or devices must be able to read such a file format. The PDF version of an e-book is popular, because it looks similar to that of a paper book, but on electronic media. The users can make notes, bookmark the pages, highlight the texts, and copy, paste, save, and print selected texts. In addition to these, some e-book readers also include varying font styles, as well as dictionaries within them. The names of a few aggregators and publishers who produce e-books include: OCLC NetLibrary, Questia, Ebook Library, University Press, ebray, and Sage Publications, etc.

2.2.13 Institutional Repository

An Institutional Repository (IR) is the intellectual output of a university or institution in the form of digital collections. The scholarly printed and published materials written by faculty members or research staff of institutions are made available to users worldwide, through web-based searchable databases available on the internet or intranet. The institutional repositories help improve scholarly communication, and disseminate the outputs of research works of specific organizations to the community at large. An IR could be anything from a student thesis and project reports, faculty's publications, to lecture notes and presentations, etc. Taking into consideration both privacy and intellectual property issues, content could include e-prints, preprints, technical reports, course outlines, data sets, and symposia proceedings. A number of software applications have been developed for the management of IR on the web. They include names like: DSpace, Greenstone, eScholarship, ePrints, Fedora, Dispute, Bepress, CDSware, CONTENTdm, etc.

2.2.14 Emerging Types of Electronic Resources

Listed below are emerging e-resource types that take unconventional and innovative routes to handle information, and hold considerable potential for libraries as well.

2.2.14.1 Blogs

Blogs are personal diaries where the entries and events are listed in reverse chronological order. They have a very simply format, and do not have very stringent patterns of writing. Thus, they have revolutionized the concept of web publishing. Other readers can also record their comments and concerns on the blogs.

2.2.14.2 Wikis: Editable Websites

Wikis have been with us for a few years as well, and are probably best known for the Wikipedia project. It seems likely that they, alongside blogs and Really-Simple-Syndication (RSS), will have a significant impact on libraries in the next decade. Wikis are a useful tool for facilitating online education. They can also be considered helpful for the creation and delivery of user-generated documentation for work groups and teams, since these are places where blogs and wikis are maintained to track progress reports.

2.2.14.3 Really-Simple-Syndication Feeds

Really-Simple-Syndication or Rich Site Summary (RSS) is an "XML text-based data format containing a list of items, each typically with a title, summary, URL link, and date" [21]. Its main purpose is to alert users to any future changes and modifications that have been made within the core document or the source. Libraries can use RSS feeds as an easy means of publicizing activities, developments, and other library-related news. RSS feeds give us the ability to subscribe to various services and link to other users. RSS can be used to disseminate news, events, or summary information on a particular topic. Google docs and spreadsheets, blogs and wikis are capable of generating an RSS feed.

2.2.14.4 Shared Bookmarking: "Social Classification" or "Folksonomies"

This offers libraries a new tool, although, almost by definition, they are possibly of more use to personal users. It allows users to store bookmarks online.

2.3 ADVANTAGES OF ELECTRONIC RESOURCES

1. Accessible and Searchable: E-resources can be accessed on/off the campus 24 × 7 and are easily searched with advance search techniques which are quick and can be used for easy pinpointing. Full-text search of e-resources can also be done via an online index.

2. Interactive: Articles available in e-resources can be read, commented on, and amended quickly by readers, and also can receive feedback through the web.
3. Links and Alerts: The hypertext format provides links to relevant articles and important websites, as well as constant URLs for particular articles. The latest issues loaded/published alert the users/readers through e-mail and other modes.
4. Inexpensive: Electronic resources are cheaper than printed materials with regard to printing and distribution costs. Electronic formats alleviate the staff and facility costs associated with material shelving and storage, both in current stack areas and in storage facility.
5. Flexibility: E-journals evolve quickly. They are not tied to or regulated by a particular format, printer, or distribution network.

2.4 DISADVANTAGES OF ELECTRONIC RESOURCES

1. Discomfort in reading from the screen or poor graphic quality.
2. Access to e-resources require knowledge of computer and internet skills on the part of the users.
3. Depending upon the internet speed, e-resources can be accessed and downloaded.
4. Perishable Citation: Once online, if a website changes, the URL citations disappear.
5. Authenticity: Authors concerned about establishing the source and authority of material in general, find it hard to convince the reader of their credibility.
6. While searching through the web for a particular e-resource, a deluge of related information appears against the search. This makes it difficult to choose the right ones from the useless ones.
7. It is tough to decide when one should stop searching the required information and start writing. This leads to procrastination, as one keeps on looking through information, making it difficult to get started with the writing stuff by holding a particular end.
8. There are chances that the quality of work that one wishes to develop may go down because of the elaborate and taxing search through what is legitimate information and what is not.

2.5 ELECTRONIC RESOURCE MANAGEMENT

Electronic resources play an emerging role in libraries on many levels. The incessant intensification of e-resources available in variety, e.g., full-text databases, bibliographic databases, e-books, e-journals, e-theses, digitized and born-digital documents, digital images, streaming video sound, and audio books, become more difficult to manage effectively. These e-resources increase the challenge for an information professional to adequately access, as well as manage, the diverse body of e-resources available. Because of such growing challenges, it is essential to have a "one-stop solution" to manage all of them. Electronic Resource Management System (ERMS) is the perfect solution that caters to the need for evaluation, selection, acquisition, renewal/cancelation, license agreements, access rights, usage statistics, single access point, copyright, implementation, and administration of e-resources. Electronic Resource Management (ERM) software assists the libraries to manage the details of the e-resources that are accessed as well as managed.

According to Breeding [22], there are two aspects of managing electronic resources. They are:

1. The front-end details of delivering the content to library users; and
2. Managing the business details of back-end staff functions that are related to acquisition, payment, and licensing [22].

The process involved in managing e-resources, i.e., the lifecycle of e-resources, starts from evaluation, trial, selection, license agreements, acquisition, access, and administration, and concludes at support service, evolution monitor, and renewal or cancelation. The tool used for managing the lifecycle of e-resources is called ERMS, which is basically designed for library professionals, but also impacts end-users.

2.6 EVOLUTION OF ELECTRONIC RESOURCE MANAGEMENT

With the influx of e-resources, most libraries found that the collection, operation, and service of these new e-resources were very difficult to manage with their existing Integrated Library Management Systems (ILMS). A study made by Jewell in 2001 stated that many libraries had started developing local software to beat these pitfalls. The workshop held in May 2002 in Chicago cosponsored by NISO (National Information Standards Organization) and the Digital Library Federation (DLF) discussed standards related to issues of ERMS. This led to the formation of

DLFs Electronic Resource Management Initiative (ERMI) in October 2002, and a published report known as the ERMI Report in August 2004 [23].

The report asserted the need for "comprehensive ERMs," and also followed a review of several locally-developed ERMS that identified the following set of goals for the initiative:

1. Design and develop universal tools and specifications to manage the license agreements and internal administrative processes which are associated with licensed electronic resources;
2. Depict architectures required for e-resource management;
3. Promote the development of systems.

The ERMI steering group also observed that the challenge that had to be immediately addressed is support for the lifecycle of electronic resources, including selection and acquisition, access provision, resource administration, user support, troubleshooting (staff and end-users), and renewal and retention decisions. To facilitate this, the report provided a number of closely-related documents, including a data dictionary that encompassed a wide range of data elements (administrative information, license permissions, contacts for troubleshooting and support, user IDs and passwords, price caps and cancelation restrictions, etc.). The data dictionary was supported and further elaborated upon by a "data structure" document and an entity relationship diagram. In addition to the above, a full set of functional requirements, and a set of flowcharts were also designed to depict processes that need to be supported by an ERM— such as mounting trials, routing licenses, placing orders, implementing access, and notifying relevant staff, were provided. Together, these documents constituted the "ERMI Spec," which was given credit by many who actually helped in launching a new application along with a set of defined services [24]. The report also identified a number of outstanding issues, such as consortium support and functionality, usage data handling and reporting, and data standards—including serials description and holdings, standard identifiers, license term expressions, and interoperability. These considerations led to the launch of an ERMI 2 project [25], also under DLF auspices, which undertook several subprojects. Two of these developed into what are now the NISO SUSHI and CORE projects. In addition, training and materials in support of "license mapping"—the practice of analyzing and encoding license terms for incorporation into ERMS—were provided to participants in four workshops that were offered as part of the project. An effort to review the ERMI data structure documents and data dictionary was also identified as part of the initiative, but could not be pursued at the time due to competing commitments on the part of those most able to undertake it [24].

In this chapter, an attempt has been made to give an overview of the major developments taking place in a library ranging from e-resources to an e-resource management system. A common understanding of e-resources, e-resources management and its evolution, and an e-resource management system has been made for the ease of the librarian, as well as for the library users.

REFERENCES

[1] Allword.com, Definition of electronic resource: Online dictionary, language guide, foreign language and etymology, n.d. Retrieved July 18, 2014, from http://www.all-words.com/word-electronic + resource.html.

[2] S. Sukula, Electronic Resource Management: What, Why and How, Ess Ess Publications, New Delhi, 2010.

[3] IFLA, ISBD(ER): International Standard Bibliographic Description for Electronic Resource, Revised from the ISBD (CF): International standard bibliographic description for computer files, 1999.

[4] K.G. Saur, ISBD(ER): International Standard Bibliographic Description for Electronic Resource: Revised From the ISBD(CF), International Standard Bibliographic Description for Computer Files, Vol. 17, K.G. Saur, Washington, DC, 1997, UBCIM Publications.

[5] C. Armstrong, R. Lonsdale, A general overview of the e-resource industry, in: G. Stone (Ed.), The E-Resources Management Handbook, UKSG., Newbury, 2011, pp. 1—16.

[6] G. Tara, 2009. Retrieved January 5, 2014, from http://www.carteret.edu/library/PPT/Electronic%20Resources.

[7] Librarian...educator...historian...entrepreneur, 2006. NextSpace, 3, 2—7.

[8] K.L. Horny, Online catalogs: coping with the choices, J. Acad. Librarianship 8 (1) (1982) 14—19.

[9] K. Antelman, E. Lynema, A.K. Pace, Toward a 21st century library catalog, Inf. Technol. Libraries 25 (3) (2006) 128—139.

[10] A.I. Moghaddam, Databases: from paper-based to web-based, 2009. Retrieved May 15, 2015, from http://digitalcommons.unl.edu/libphilprac/247/.

[11] J. Feather, R.P. Sturges, International Encyclopedia of Information and Library Science, Taylor & Francis, Boca Raton, FL, 2003.

[12] S. Bjorner, S.C. Ardito, Online before the internet, part 3: Early pioneers tell their stories: Carlos Cuadra, Searcher 11 (6) (2003) 36—46.

[13] D. Hawthorne, History of electronic resources, in: H. Yu, S. Breivold (Eds.), Electronic resource management in libraries: Research and practice, Information Science Publishing, Hershey, 2011, pp. 1—15.

[14] S. Nicholson, Introduction to web databases, 2002. Retrieved May 15. 2014, from http://www.askscott.com/sec1.html.

[15] C.G. Doe, A look at web-based databases and search tools, Inf. Today, Inc 11 (5) (2004). Retrieved July 20, 2014 from http://www.infotoday.com/mmschools/sep04/doe.shtml.

[16] R.E. Wyllys, LIS 386.13 information technologies and the information professions: Web-based databases, 2003. Retrieved July 13, 2015 from http://www.gslis.utexas.edu/~l38613dw/powerpoint/38613WebDatabases.ppt.

[17] J. Feiler, Database-Driven Web Sites, Elsevier Science & Technology Books, Philadelphia, USA, 1999.

[18] R.P. Majumder, S. Roy, E-journals license and agreements: Some issues and practical overview. *Digital Media and Library Information services*. Paper presented at the XXVI all India conference of IASLIC, Dr. Zakir Husain Library (Central Library), 2007. Jamia MilliaIslamia, New Delhi, p. 370.

[19] M. Lebert, *A Short History of Ebooks,* 2009. Retrieved June 13, 2014, from http://www.gutenberg.org/ebooks/29801.

[20] J.O. Borchers, Electronic books: definition, genres, interaction design patterns. In Conference on Human Factors in Computing Systems, CHI9 Workshop: Designing Electronic Books, 1999.

[21] J. Musser, T. O'Reilly, Web 2.0: Principles and Best Practices, O'Reilly Media, Sebastopol, CA, 2007.

[22] M. Breeding, The many facets of managing electronic resources, Comput. Libraries Westport 24 (1) (2004) 25—33.

[23] T.D. Jewell, I. Anderson, A. Chandler, S.E. Farb, K. Parker, N.D. Robertson, Electronic Resource Management. The Report of the DLF Initiative. Washington, DC: Digital Library Federation, 2004. Retrieved July 18, 2015, from http://www.diglib.org/pubs/dlf102.

[24] T. Jewell, J. Aipperspach, I. Anderson, D. England, R. Kasprowski, B. McQuillan, et al., Making Good on the Promise of ERM: A Standards and Best Practices Discussion Paper, NISO, Baltimore, 2012. Retrieved July 17, 2014, from http://www.niso.org/apps/group_public/download.php/7946.

[25] T. Jewell, DLF Electronic Resource Management Initiative, Phase II: Final Report, Digital Library Federation and Council on Library and Information Resources, Washington, DC, 2008. Retrieved July 17, 2014, from http://old.diglib.org/standards/ERMI2_Final_Report_20081230.pdf.

CHAPTER 3

Lifecycle of Electronic Resource Management

3.1 LIFECYCLE OF ELECTRONIC RESOURCE MANAGEMENT

There are five major components in the lifecycle of electronic resources management, such as: (1) acquisition management, (2) access management, (3) administration management, (4) support management, and (5) evaluation monitor management. The lifecycle of e-resources with different stages is depicted in Fig. 3.1. The five components, including their subcomponents, are described in detail below.

3.2 ACQUISITION MANAGEMENT

Before acquiring any resource in a library, the very first questions that librarians have in mind are the *why*, *what*, and *how*. These are addressed in a collection development document. A clear and effective collection development document has three distinct parts: philosophy, policy, and procedure. The philosophy underlies the *why* this collection exists. Once it is known why this collection is essential, it is then time to get to the nitty-gritty of *what* the collection is, which covers policy. The final part of the collection development document comprises of a set of procedures that are used for selecting, as well as deselecting, collections. This is the "who does what, when, and how" part of the document [1].

3.2.1 Access Need/Budget

If an e-resource is recommended for purchase, the first step should always be to assess the requirement for it, and then take a look at the allotted budget.

3.2.2 Selection, Trial, and Evaluation

A collection development policy makes it easier to select and add e-resources by selectors. Such a policy provides a skeleton for making

Digital Disruption and Electronic Resource Management in Libraries.
DOI: http://dx.doi.org/10.1016/B978-0-08-102045-6.00003-0

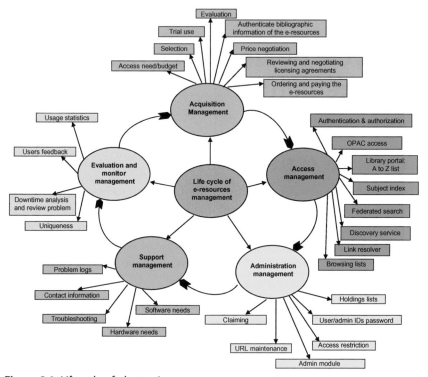

Figure 3.1 Lifecycle of electronic resource management.

consistent and informed decisions, which is very necessary for making a good plan. It is like a blueprint for the selectors, and helps them to ensure uniformity in procedures, as well as appropriate balance in the library collections. As a library needs more and more e-resources, it is necessary to integrate them into the library's overall policy. The three main purposes of a collection development policy include informing, directing, and protecting [2]. There is a three-step process for the selection of any e-resources, which includes identification/discovery, evaluation, and finally the decision to select the product [3].

There are a variety of tools that are used for the identification and discovery of e-resources which include recommendations of faculty members, research staff, librarians, trial offers, demonstrations from publishers/vendors, user recommendations, discussion lists, peer library websites, publisher's catalogue, information from other libraries of a similar nature, colleagues suggestions, etc.

After identification/discovery, in the case of paid-based e-resources, it is highly advisable for librarians to make the resources available for trial access from publishers/vendors before a purchase is made. The process of trial access gives the opportunity to the librarian and the selection committee to evaluate the e-resources in terms of consistency, uniformity, functionality, and other technical issues, by getting feedback from the users. Normally, most publishers offer a trial for a limited period of time, i.e., for a few weeks or a couple of months. Some renowned publishers who offer trials are Elsevier, EBSCO, ProQuest, etc.

Evaluation of the e-resources is the most important step for the librarian/selection committee once the resources have been identified. There are several criteria for the evaluation of e-resources, but some of the essential ones are as follows:

Content: The first step calls for reviewing and evaluating the content present within the e-resources to investigate areas like full-text, bibliographic citations, availability of retrospective material, annotations, statistically and graphically explained data, for the better guidance of users. These are generally based on the curriculum of the research work of the users.

Updates: To find out the frequency of updates, content embargos, and archiving availability is another part of the evaluation of e-resources.

Quality: Evaluation is essential to investigate the reputation of a publisher, and find out about their intellectual level, along with the quality of information they are offering.

Indexing Upgrades: Upgrades should be done to keep track of the e-resources, as well as the frequency of their indexing.

Authority: It is important to consider that e-resources should be authoritative. Evaluate whether a particular resource is scholarly or not. In the case of journals, the impact factor (i.e., its citation rating) should be considered.

Accessibility: The evaluator should also consider that the product should be easily accessible for users. The various interfaces such as the possibility of customization, stability, availability of a thesaurus, downloading options (e-mailing/printing), searching options such as Boolean, and proximity, field-specificity, etc., should be looked into while evaluating the e-resources.

Cost Factor: Cost considerations for e-resources are the most confusing part. For products like monographs and periodicals, costs vary according to the number of simultaneous users/ports/passwords, remote access, and so forth. The pricing plans, though, are not standardized between vendors, but may be standardized for individual vendors. Content providers may offer special deals for consortia members as a whole, and the pricing varies based on full-time enrollment, materials budget, authentication of users, simultaneous use, and remote access for users [3].

Technical Support: Evaluation should consider the technical support of the service provider for the products. Technical support may include a staff training program and online help, as well as detailed help pages for the users of the product which are compatible with existing hardware and software.

Licensing Agreement: Though reviewing a license agreement is not considered a selector's job, it is important to carefully consider the general agreement such as various restrictions, access to archived information, definition of authorized users, use for distance education, off-campus access, and availability of usage statistics [3].

The above-mentioned evaluation criteria is a tool for the librarian/ selection committee of e-resources for making a final selection decision which is commensurate with the increasing costs and decreasing budgets of the library. The decision should be carefully and consciously taken for each resource, so that the institute's vision can be met.

3.2.3 Authenticate Bibliographic Information of the Electronic Resources

After the final decision about the product is made by the selector, the first step in acquiring the e-resources is to verify its detailed bibliographic information, such as coverage, content provider of the product, frequency of updates, and cost.

3.2.4 Price Negotiation

There is a lack of a standard pricing model to negotiate the pricing of e-resources. The price varies from product to product, considering the range of the pricing models. It should be used for determining which models are the best to meet the timely requirements of the library. The following are common pricing models, which are not limited to:

1. Product Type: Aggregator database, full-text databases.
2. Product available through yearly subscription, one-time purchase, or multiyear deals with fixed price caps.

3. Rental models.
4. Print plus electronic deal.
5. Institution size (some vendors charge more when selling to a large organization with multiple branches, locations, or sites compared to small sized organizations).
6. Number of users (full-time equivalents of students, total number of students, staff, and faculty, unlimited access including remote access).
7. Price for consortia deal.
8. Price for journal package deals (bundle sets of title in an electronic journal package).
9. Price for content access (full-text article, or abstract and indexing database).
10. Patron-Driving Acquisition models, e.g., purchase of e-resources based on usage by patrons, including numbers of downloads, views, or length of use of the items [4].

3.2.5 Reviewing and Negotiating Licensing Agreements

One of the most critical issues of acquisition of e-resources relates to dealing with license agreements. Once the procurement of the e-resources has been decided, the license agreement for the product must be reviewed and negotiated. The license agreement contains various clauses and terms that define the rights of the libraries, users, and publishers/content providers. The following are the vital terms/clauses that librarians may review and use for negotiating the license agreements of the products.

3.2.5.1 Authorized Users and Sites

The "authorized users" clause includes students, staff, faculty, and research scholars, whereas the clause "authorized sites" states the name of the sites/premises that should have authorized access to the product. Authorized users can access the licensed resources from a particular building/campus/office, from a remote location through an Internet Protocol (IP) authenticated protocol system/use of a proxy server, through remote access, or through a user ID and password. It thus permits multiple users to access e-resources at the same time from different geographical locations.

3.2.5.2 Archiving Policy and Perpetual Access

The publisher should mention the archiving and perpetual access policy for the e-resources. The perpetual access clause allows a library to retain certain e-resources where payment has been made, even after termination of an agreement.

3.2.5.3 Institutional/Self-Archiving

This clause allows the author and the institution to upload their publications to institutional repositories in preprint or postprint format.

3.2.5.4 Copyright and Fair User

This clause allows users to view, download, or print material. Some other services, such as permission for interlibrary loan through document transmission systems like Ariel or other similar protocols, electronic course reserve, distance education, course packages, etc., may be allowed.

3.2.5.5 Usage Statistics

Content providers should agree to provide usage statistics for e-resources accessed by the library's users.

3.2.5.6 Liability for Unauthorized Use

It is the responsibility of the library to monitor and mark out unauthorized users.

3.2.5.7 Privacy and Confidentiality

This clause requires the guarantee of privacy and confidentiality for the user's accessing information of e-resources. The information is generally accessed through their created personal account.

3.2.5.8 Cost

Cost of the e-resources should be mentioned in the agreement.

3.2.5.9 Technical Considerations

The content provider should address some technical considerations in the license agreement. He/she should indicate whether the content of the e-resources are available via link resolver, open URL, or link server. Content offered by the content provider should have consistency. Metadata of e-resources should be provided for the integration in the Library's OPAC, Discovery tools, and Federated search. Contact information of the content provider should be mentioned for the purpose of technical and customer support. Electronic resources should be accessible by various web browsers, such as Netscape, Chrome, opera, Internet Explorer, Mozilla, Safari, etc. Online help screens or online user document manuals should be provided. During the licensing period, there should be a guarantee of more than 99% uptime to the e-resources, any interruption to access should lead to a deduction in the license fee, or extension of the license period that is commensurable to the amount of downtime. E-resources should be provided with a digital object identifier for a stable link to the information in the resources.

3.2.5.10 Suppleness and Improvement

Some issues should be addressed by the content provider in the license agreement, such as there should be provision for shifting from the existing print version to the e-version. The visual quality of e-resources should be same or better than the print version. The price of the e-resources should be the same in comparison with the print version. The license agreement should be reviewed and renewed/canceled every year, at the beginning of each calendar year or fiscal year, with prior advance notice.

3.2.5.11 Indemnification

This clause states that one or both parties should not be financially responsible for any monetary loss.

3.2.5.12 Terms of Payment and Termination

Payment liability should be started from the date of access of the licensed e-resources. A termination appeal would be granted only after knowing the reason for and time of termination, and receiving a notification from the provider.

3.2.5.13 Governing Law

Any disputes in the license agreement should be settled within the geographical limits of the institution.

3.2.6 Ordering and Paying for the Electronic Resources

There is not much difference between ordering for and paying for e-resources from the process for print resources. After reviewing the license agreement and signing it, the following steps should be followed for acquiring the e-resources.

1. Communicate with the content provider about the e-resource that is being signed for, and request provision of an ID or password, or allow access through an IP address.
2. The content provider provides a stable URL for the product, through which the resources can be accessed.
3. Verify access to the products and inform departments about the availability of the new resource.
4. Notifyvarious library departments, such as cataloguing, technology, collection development, to add the e-resources in OPAC, intranet page/library portal, Discovery, etc.
5. Schedule training on e-resources.
6. After access is confirmed, the provider must send an invoice for payment.
7. Review the invoice to ensure that the charges have been included as per agreement.
8. Process the payment by credit card, or authorize an invoice to be paid by the institution's accounting, accounts payable, or procurement department, depending on the institute's procurement rules.

3.3 ACCESS MANAGEMENT

After the procurement of e-resources, the most important function of any modern library is to provide access to or display of those e-resources in an acceptable manner to cater to the organization's needs. Here, technical details of setting up access and different online access tools are discussed which are considered as part of an overall access management system pertaining to e-resources.

3.3.1 Authentication and Authorization

There are various mechanisms for both authentication and authorization of licensed e-resources. Authentication is the process of validating the identity of authorized users including faculty members, staff, students, and other library users, as defined within the licensed agreement. The most popular authentication options are username and password-based access, IP, and remote access. Before talking about authentication options, it is important to know about the authentication sources, such as API (Application Programming Interface) and LDAP (Lightweight Directory Access Protocol). Both API and LDAP are available in all major programming languages. It is simple for information systems such as integrated library management systems (ILMS), meta search systems, proxy server and e-mail systems, to authenticate a user. An API is a set of definitions of the ways by which one piece of computer software communicates with another, whereas LDAP is a well-established protocol for accessing personal data in a directory. The existence of such infrastructure in the organization would be ideal for a single source of authentication for library systems, as well as for other information systems [5].

The method for accessing e-resources via user ID/password becomes less secure, as it is not easy to keep the password a secret for a long period. As a consequence, IP authenticated access methods have become more popular, and are commonly used in the library, as the user does not need to remember or worry about a user ID and password. In this mechanism, a library provides a range of IP addresses to the content provider. The IP filtering should be performed by both library and service providers. Since the IP-based access authentication has a suitable and appropriate function for accessing e-resources for on-campus users, off-campuses or remote users are unable to use them. Therefore, to overcome the difficulty of both local and remote users an alternative mechanism called "remote login" and "single sign-on" (SSO), known as "reduced sign-on" (RSO) have solved the problem.

If users want to access the e-resources outside the designated IP range, then the user may be assigned a login to the database, or simply use a proxy server to access the material. A proxy server allows users with login credentials to log in to the proxy server. Here, campus networks allow remote access to authorized users by passing them through a proxy server. If users come from an IP address which is located outside the campus IP range, then it will not allow the users to investigate further without confirming their user ID and password. The user ID and password are then authenticated by campus LDAP, a system where all the user IDs and passwords are managed. This means that only authorized users can pass through the proxy.

Another system which addresses this issue is the SSO system, also known as RSO. It is a property that ensures access control by independent as well as multiple software systems. This allows users to log in once and gain access to all systems without being prompted to log in again (Wikipedia, 5 July 2013). If there is an infrastructure that allows users to log in once, and be able to access other e-resource system without being asked to log in again during the session, then it definitely has an effective SSO system, regardless of the method or technologies that have been used to accomplish it. The SSO not only provides a more convenient user experience, but also manages to make the system more secure, because of the reduced number of authentication systems used [5]. The most popular products available for this system are Central Authentication Service (CAS), Shibboleth, EZproxy, and Athens.

3.3.2 Online Public Access Catalogue Access

One of the online access tools of e-resources is OPAC, which stands for Online Public Access Catalogue, a module of ILS for displaying/searching the library's catalogue for users. Here, the library regularly uploads the MARC record or Dublin Core metadata record of e-resources. This process is labor intensive, as titles come and go from content providers on a regular basis. Again, the individual librarian may have limited or no authority to change the underlying structure of the OPAC itself, and the appearance and design of an OPAC can vary quite a bit, and still serve its fundamental purpose. What is most essential to consider is that e-resources are clearly indicated, as such in search results, because a patron's search could pull multiple results in an equal number of different formats. Second, links must be functional and sufficiently prominent to be obvious to patrons at a single glance and not easily confused with other types of links that may appear on the OPAC result page, such as widgets, help links, or other links [6].

3.3.3 Library Portal A-to-Z List

This provides access to e-resources with an A–to–Z list through library portals which contain links to all e-resources. It is the cheapest and easiest way to provide access to small holdings which are normally practiced in India. It allows the users to access e-resources easily.

3.3.4 Subject Index

With the help of this tool, e-resources can be indexed, as well as searched against a specific subject for the development of an academic discipline. Content providers who include subject indexes in their databases are EBSCO, ProQuest, J-Gate, Elsevier, Emerald, etc.

3.3.5 Federated Search

Federated search is also known as meta search, poly search, or broadcast search. Instead of searching the e-resource one by one in different platforms, it allows users to opt for real-time search of multiple e-resources simultaneously through a single search query. Here, users can get the search result through an integrated list. Some names of good products available in the market include Research Pro from Innovative Interfaces, 360 search from Serials Solutions, MetaLib from Ex Libris, Google Scholar from Google, and EBSCOhost Integrated Search from EBSCO.

3.3.6 Discovery Service

This also refers to a discovery layer. Discovery service preindexes the metadata and also the full-text documents, whereas federated search applications basically search live sources. As the data are preindexed, discovery services retrieve results quickly [7]. The federated search products rely on connectors and go for remote searches, but these solutions are only partial and limited. Discovery services provide a single search interface to multiple resources. It uses a centralized consolidated index, and provides better and faster search results [8]. Discovery service is a single interface which searches the preindexed metadata and/or full-text documents of all e-resources, both internal (library) and external (content provider/databases, vendors/open source, etc.). Since the metadata are preindexed and harvested in a single server, the search result of discovery service is received more quickly than a federated search. Products available for discovery service are EBSCO's discovery service, Serial Solutions' Summon, Ex Libris' Primo, Innovative Interfaces' Encore, SirsiDynix Enterprise, etc.

3.3.7 Link Resolver

This allows users to find out the availability of scholarly full-text information resources such as e-books, e-journals, e-theses, etc., that the library have and redirects the users to those resources. According to SHARPA *Glossary of Open Access Abbreviations, Acronyms and Terms* the link resolver is "a service that directs users from a public online link to content that the user has a right to read, normally by virtue of institutionally subscribed resources." Link resolver works or does not work to the degree that a given information resource is OpenURL compliant, otherwise known as NISO/ANSI standard Z39.88. To put it simply, OpenURL is a standard format of URL that enables users to find an appropriate copy of a given resource while searching a database or other discovery tool; more specifically in the case of libraries, an article or other full-text resource that users of a specific library have the license to access. Link resolvers parse the element of an OpenURL, and then provide links to appropriate copies or targets that are available from the library's holdings [6]. Common types of link resolvers used by libraries rely on the OpenURL framework. Some examples of link resolvers are Ex libris' SFX (also listed as an A-to-Z list), Innovative Interfaces' WebBridge, EBSCO's LinkSource, etc.

3.3.8 Browsing List

In this tool list of e-resources, there are certain multiple or interrelated web pages organized in an alphabetical manner and usually developed by using HTML, PHP, and CSS. For this, libraries may create their own web pages, or may use a proprietary product such as LibGuides. LibGuide is a web-based knowledge sharing system designed with a librarian's mind for showcasing high quality research information to users, even if the users did not know they existed.

3.4 ADMINISTRATION MANAGEMENT

In this component of lifecycle of e-resources, librarians/electronic resource professionals should have the administrative power for configuration and customization, and should monitor the different functions of the administration module for the content provider/vendor's website or other ERM systems. Librarians should know how functionality and access to e-resources are configured using these modules. Some functions of administration management discussed below.

3.4.1 Knowledge Base/Holdings

A knowledge base is a database of information that holds library e-resources. It contains metadata of e-resources that can be identified and maintain appropriate coverage and URLs per title while also supporting holdings display in the catalogue. It is also required to update the holding list of e-resources if modified or changed.

3.4.2 User/Admin IDs Password

Admin user ID and password should be made available to the authorized users. User IDs to the end user interface may exist, and may need to be changed and managed efficiently with time. At the very least, the user ID to the administrative site needs to be recorded and/or "remembered."

3.4.3 Access Restriction

In this administration module, features like restriction to access of a number of concurrent users, user location, etc., should be present. Information regarding whether a user can download material or use the items in course packs, or satisfy interlending request, etc., should also be available.

3.4.4 Admin Module Information

This is the central control of all the components/modules of a system. The most important function of the admin module is to control/prevent the already setting parameters from someone else. Permission for use of the admin module must be given to those persons who are authorized for e-resource management. The information provided could be tracked within this module, which has the URL to the administrative module along with their username and password. Besides these, other settings include loaded holdings, OpenURL, and many more.

3.4.5 URL Maintenance

Sometimes URL to e-resources may change, and this needs to be modified/changed where e-resources are linked to prevent the loss of access.

3.4.6 Claiming

Claiming is what a librarian would be doing when they intend to track down an e-resource, but have lost access to it, or if they think that an issue should be online but it is not. It is still the case that publishers sometimes promise to deliver online content but do not, as sometimes publications are delayed for months or years. When this happens, libraries do not want to be paying for the product. This is not to say that discovery of missing content and claiming it is an easy task (often it is based on reports from end users rather than a regular process), but the need remains.

3.4.7 Support Management

Support management for e-resources involves several functions which are provided below.

3.4.7.1 Problem Logs

The support management system is responsible for addressing logging problems with resources as well as content providers. There should be a "web-based problem logging form" for users to submit issues they are facing with e-resources. After submission of the problem through this form, e-mails should be generated for each problem and sent to e-resource librarians. Next, its logs should have entries in the online problem log. Then the e-resource librarian can visit the log and notify the problem as "Under Process" or "Resolved," with a textbox to explain the situation. This will help users, content providers, and e-resource librarians get the report of the problem so that a content provider can track the frequency of the problem, and the e-resource librarian can evaluate the e-resources at the time of renewal/cancelation by keeping record of the downtime.

3.4.7.2 Contact Information

The contact information, such as e-mail, phone, snail mail address, etc., of users, content providers, vendors, and tech support personnel should be available to a communicating person at the right time.

3.4.7.3 Troubleshooting

Unlike print resources, e-resources address a variety of issues and problems which require troubleshooting and technical support. But, there are certain problems that one faces while accessing e-resources. They could be one or more numbers of things ranging between anything from human errors in date range availability, change in URL, problems with the proxy server, changed or altered IP addresses that have not been reported to the provider, down the performance of a publisher's site, etc. Keeping this in view, a set of troubleshooting guidelines should be available in the system. It is also important for e-resource management professionals to know what type of issues he/she can solve, and what type of issues must be delegated to either internal organization information technology (IT) professionals or external vendor or publisher-based IT professionals.

3.4.7.4 Hardware and Software

It is important to note that some products may have special hardware and software needs, e.g., while some which may not work well on a MAC operating system, may work on others that are available in the market.

3.5 EVALUATION AND MONITOR MANAGEMENT

Evaluation and monitoring management is the final step in the e-resources lifecycle. This step results in the renewal of the e-resources for another year, a multiyear contract, or even cancelation of the e-resources. To get the desired results, there are certain evaluation tools, discussed below.

3.5.1 Usage Statistics

Usage statistics are the best tool to appraise the performance of e-resources. The preference should be facilitated to generate the usage statistics title wise, database wise, and publisher wise on all the paid-based and open source e-resources that include the institutional repository and library catalogue available through OPAC, etc. With complete information about this usage, it becomes easier for librarians to evaluate the cost-effectiveness or per use of the resources. To get the usage statistics, new standards and technologies have been developed, such as COUNTER and SUSHI. COUNTER stands for Counting Online Usage of Networked Electronic Resources. It was launched in March 2002. It is simply an initiative which caters to the need of publishers, librarians, and intermediaries by setting a certain standard that would facilitate the consistent reporting of online usage statistics [9]. COUNTER helps in usage statistics. The problem with COUNTER is that usage has to be gathered file by file from the various publishers' sites. COUNTER specifically denotes precisely how to lay out the usage report. But there are some discrepancies, and hence the efficiency of the whole model has to be improved. Some other e-resource management modules include usage consolidation applications. The library loads the vendor's COUNTER reports to a database from which consolidated reports can be generated. But as there are lots of online vendors/publishers it takes a lot of time to gather the reports. To overcome this issue, SUSHI (Standardized Usage Statistics Harvesting Initiative) was initiated [10]. SUSHI is an automated request and response model for generating usage data which utilizes a web services framework. It replaces the time-consuming user mediated gathering of usage data reports, and retrieves varieties of usage reports. SUSHI is built on SOAP (Simple Object Access Protocol) for transferring request and response messages [9].

3.5.2 Users Feedback

Feedback and useful input from users is a great tool for evaluation of the nature of the e-resources and ensuring their renewal/cancelation. User's feedback may include the relevance and quality of content, research on campus and the curriculum, usability of e-resources, etc.

3.5.3 Downtime Analysis and Review Problems

Review of downtime time and/or problem logs should be analyzed before renewing the e-resources. If the system or content provider site gives maximum downtime, then there is no point renewing it even if the content is beneficial.

3.5.4 Uniqueness

The uniqueness of the resources can be evaluated by comparing duplication in various formats or overlapping in full-text resources. Individual titles in a publisher's package generally cannot be canceled. Sometimes, the titles are duplicated in aggregator databases, which do not provide stable access and hence require renewal of the subscription [3].

For any library, it is important to ensure application of lifecycle/workflow for e-resource management. If libraries follow the complete procedure of workflow, they would be in a position to manage their e-resources better, and eventually cut down on additional expenses over e-resources. This would, in turn, save a lot of time and get the required information. The basic principles of the criteria/methods for each component of e-resources have been addressed, which may be very useful for the library professionals in managing the e-resources.

REFERENCES

[1] K. Wikoff, Electronics Resources Management in the Academic Library: A Professional Guide, Libraries Unlimited, Santa Barbara, CA, 2012.
[2] V.L. Gregory, A. Hanson, Selecting and Managing Electronic Resources: A How-to-do-it Manual for Librarian, Neal-Schuman Publishers, New York, 2006.
[3] S. Joshipura, Selecting, acquiring, and renewing electronic resources, in: H. Yu, S. Breivold (Eds.), Electronic Resource Management in Libraries: Research and Practice, Information Science Publishing, Hershey, 2008, pp. 46−65.
[4] S. Johnson, O.G. Evensen, J. Gelfand, G. Lammers, L. Sipe, N. Zilper, Key Issues for E-resource Collection Development: A Guide for Libraries, IFLA, 2012.

[5] J.C. Rodriguez, B. Zhang, Authentication and access management of electronic resources, in: H. Yu, S. Breivold (Eds.), Electronic Resource Management in Libraries: Research and Practice, Information Science Publishing, Hershey, 2008, pp. 250–274.

[6] G. Stachokas, Managing electronic resources accessible, in: Ryan O. Weir (Ed.), Managing Electronic Resources: A LITA Guide, ALATechSource, Chicago, 2012, pp. 69–85.

[7] Sol, Discovering discovery services, 2009. Retrieved July 14, 2014 from http://federatedsearchblog.com/2009/07/19/discovering-discovery-services.

[8] Hane, P.J., New Discovery tools for online resources from OCLC and EBSCO, 2009. Retrieved July, 14, 2013 from http://newsbreaks.infotoday.com/NewsBreaks/New-Discovery-Tools-for-Online-Resources-From-OCLC-and-EBSCO-53468.asp.

[9] Standardized usage statistics harvesting initiative (SUSHI), n.d. Retrieved July 14, 2014 from http://www.niso.org/workrooms/sushi.

[10] O. Pesch, Usage statistics: about COUNTER and SUSHI, Inf. Serv. Use 27 (4) (2007) 207–213.

CHAPTER 4

An Electronic Resource Management System and Its Best Practice

4.1 ELECTRONIC RESOURCE MANAGEMENT SYSTEMS

Electronic Resource Management Systems (ERMS) are used "... to keep track of a library's digital titles, subscription and vendor/publisher information, and link resolution with more accuracy and less duplication" [1]. ERMS are systems designed to manage the details involved in the acquisition of e-resources, including subscription and licensing details, usage, cost, access tracking, and data gathering. In general, an ERMS is used for record keeping and budgeting activities, while Content Management Systems are used for access and authority control. In certain cases, these functions can overlap. There are several good and stand-alone commercial, as well as open source ERMS, that are available today. There are also many ILS (Integrated Library Systems) that integrate some form of ERMS in their functionality [2,3].

In 2002, the Digital Library Federation (DLF) and the National Information Standards Organization (NISO) cosponsored a workshop that eventually led to the Electronic Resource Management Initiative (ERMI). The landmark ERMI report, published in 2004 [4], articulated the challenges of e-resource management and stands as a model that companies and individuals building new ERMS can follow. The original work of the ERMI evolved into ERMI, Phase II, which continued to explore the varied issues associated with e-resource management, such as data standards and usage statistics [5]. Bob McQuillan noted in a January 12, 2011, presentation at an NISO webinar [6] that the challenges faced by e-resource librarians were essentially fourfold. E-resource data had existed in several different formats, which were mainly not centralized. Thus, data was often stored and accessed in a variety of silos, and was left unintegrated within the ILS. So, to what extent have we solved these challenges, and what are the obstacles that have remained [7]?

Digital Disruption and Electronic Resource Management in Libraries.
DOI: http://dx.doi.org/10.1016/B978-0-08-102045-6.00004-2

ERMS are a one-stop solution for e-resource management which contain two parts, including "management" and "access" for both librarians and end-users, and compliance with specific standards and compatibility.

Several companies/vendors/institutions have developed ERM products. Some of the commercial and open-source products are mentioned below.

4.1.1 Commercial Products

1. Innovative ERM: Innovation Interfaces, Inc.
2. TDNet ERM Solutions: TDNetInc.
3. Alma ERM: Ex Libris.
4. Web-share License Manager: OCLC.
5. 360 Resource Manager: Serials Solutions.
6. Gold Rush: Colorado Alliance of Research Libraries.
7. EBSCONET ERM Essential: EBSCO.
8. E-Resource Central: SIRSI.

4.1.2 Open Source Products

1. The Semper Tool Digital Library Suite (DLS): SemperTool.
2. CORAL: University of Notre Dame's Hesburgh Libraries.

A comparison analysis of the above 10 ERMS has been made of their modules, features, standards, workflow management, etc., that have been implemented within the software. Information has been taken from the websites of the ERM companies, as well as from articles published from different sources. Table 4.1 represents the comparison of 10 ERMS on functionality, use of standards and compatibility, distinguish features and modules, etc.

4.2 INNOVATIVE ELECTRONIC RESOURCE MANAGEMENT [8]

For the purpose of managing e-resources, Innovative Interface developed an Innovative ERM in the year 2004. This software offers several advantages that include a time-saving feature, collection analysis, budget centralizing, and assimilation of technical as well as administrative details of e-resources.

Table 4.1 Comparison of electronic resource management systems

Sr. No.	Name of software	Developed by	Functions/modules	Year of development	Open source/proprietary	Standards and compatibility	Platform, programming language, database	Features	URL link
1	Innovative ERM	Innovative Interface	Staff Modules Millennium Catalog MARC Report Report Writer WebBridge LR Reference Databases	2004	Proprietary	ANSI/NISO search and Retrieval Protocol, COUNTER, Excel and Text Format, MARC, ONIX and SUSHI	Linux Java PostgreSQL	It offers the Content Access Service (CASE), tools for users access such as Spell Check, RSS feeds, faceted search results, manage licenses, and coverage data.	http://www.iii.com/products/electronic_resource.shtml
2	TDNet ERM Solutions	TDNetInc	Comprehensive knowledge base, eJournal and eBook management, Holdings Manager, TOU Resolver, Searcher Analyzer, New Acquisitions Module	2000	Proprietary	COUNTER Delimited, Excel and Text format support, Full text resolver, MARC, NISO, NIX, OpenURL, SOH (Serial Online Holdings), SUSHI, XML.	NA	Flexibility of ILL, presentation of A-to-Z holdings, multilevel customization and personalization, federated searching, eBook Manager, link resolver, partners with the Copyright Clearance Center (CCC).	http://www.tdnet.io/
3	Alma ERM	Ex Libris	Cataloguing Acquisitions Resource Management Circulation Administration	2012	Proprietary	SIP2, EDI, OAI-PMH, COUNTER 4, SUSHI, NISO Circ (NCIP 2), RDA—as MARC encoded fields, MARC21, Dublin Core, MARCXML, Z39.50, ISO2709 is supported in its MARC21/UNIMARC versions, RFID—supported as part of our	Linux, Window	It supports selection, acquisition, metadata management, digitization, and fulfillment.	http://www.exlibrisgroup.com/category/AlmaOverview

(Continued)

Table 4.1 (Continued)

Sr. No.	Name of software	Developed by	Functions/ modules	Year of development	Open source/ proprietary	Standards and compatibility	Platform, programming language, database	Features	URL link
						development roadmap, KBART—we support the export and import of KBART data, ONIX—we support the import of ONIX base license data, AACR2—is supported in its MARC21 version, DCRM(B)—it is possible to catalogue all necessary characters for DCRM(B) in Alma			
4	Web-share License Manager	OCLC	Matadata, Integrated Acquisition, Licenses, Circulation, Admin.Help.	NA	Proprietary	COUNTER, Ezproxy, OCLC MARC Format, OpenURL link resolver, Z39.50 search and Retrieval Protocol	NA	Interlibrary loan, Course reserves, Archival materials, Perpetual access, Remote access, Post-cancellation access, Copying and sharing, A to Z journal list	https://www.oclc.org/license-manager.en.html
5	The Semper Tool Digital Library Suite (DLS)	SemperTool	Resource Management System, A-to-Z Products and Resources, Link Resolver Statistics, Discovery, Reports	NA	Open sources	SUSHI, GetMeThere (GMT) OpenURL based link resolver	Window, LAMP (Linux, Apache, MySQL, Perl)	Product description, Price information, Renewal notification, Subscription history, contact information of content provider, Availability holding information, File upload, Access control, General reports, Renewal	http://www.sempertool.dk/

#	Name	Institution	Features	Year	Source	Standards	OS/Technology	Description	URL
6	CORAL	University of Notre Dame's Hesburgh Libraries	Resource, Licensing, Organizations, Usage, Management	2010	Open sources	LDAP(Lightweight directory access protocol), MySQL, ONIX-PL JR1 and JR1a COUNTER	Linux, Window, Mac JavaScript, PHP5, MySQL5,	A workflow management tool	http://coral-erm.org/
7	360 Resource Manager	SerialsSolutions	Aggregate data for subscription, Holdings, Licensing, Contacts, Trial notes, Login	2005	Proprietary	COUNTER and SUSHI, CrossRef DOI Linking, MARC, NISO1, OAI-PMH, ONIX SRU/SRW, OpenURL, SOAP, SOH, XML		Consortium edition, Reporting, Data import, Collection development, Cost management, Seamless integration with discovery services, Contact manager, Resource note manager, Licence manager and terms of use, Manu manager, Resource status, Subscription metadata, Alert manager, vendor statistic manager, Overlap analysis, Account manager, Integration with 360 counter	http://www.proquest.com/products-services/360-Resource-Manager.html
8	Gold Rush	Colorado Alliance	Decision Support, A-to-Z and Link Resolver, Library Content Comparison System	2001	Proprietary	OpenURL link resolver with full compliance for NISO 1.0 and 0.1 standards, SOAP Protocol, Support Excel format, SUSHI, XML	Linux, PHP5, Perl	Open access journals that can select and add to holdings. Control as per own style sheets. Public search interface (A-to-Z), Content Comparison, create a customized interface	https://www.coalliance.org/software/gold-rush

(Continued)

Table 4.1 (Continued)

Sr. No.	Name of software	Developed by	Functions/ modules	Year of development	Open source/ proprietary	Standards and compatibility	Platform, programming language, database	Features	URL link
9	EBSCONET' ERM Essentials	EBSCO	My collection, Renewal, Upload, Reminders, Tasks, Options and Reports.	2010	proprietary	ANSI/NISO, CORE (Cost of Resource Exchange) HTML Format, MARC, ONIX, OpenURL link resolver, Support Excel format, support proxy, XML	Web-based	Integrated Knowledge Base, EBSCO's OpenURL link resolver, maintains approx. 100 highly customizable data fields for e-packages, single-point access, Create your own reports, Customize fields, hide fields that are not relevant for your processes, and create fields specifically for your library	http://www2.ebsco. com/hi-in/ ProductsServices/ ERM/Pages/ ERMInfo.aspx
10	E-Resource Central	SIRSI Corp	Vendors, Catalogue, Your users	2011		MARC, ONIX, XML	Linux, Window	E-content management	http://www.sirsidynix. com/products/ eresource-central

4.2.1 Features

- Offers a content access service.
- Provides tools for patron access such as Spell Check.
- Integrated Really-Simple-Syndication feeds.
- Faceted search results.
- Ability to maintain resources, track licenses, and manage coverage data, etc.

4.2.2 Standards and Compatibility

ANSI/NISO search and Retrieval Protocol, COUNTER, Excel and Text Format, MARC, ONIX and SUSHI, are the standards and compatibility adopted by the Innovative ERM.

4.2.3 Functions and Modules

The modules available in this software are acquisitions, serials, cataloguing, circulation, and management reports.

4.3 TDNET ELECTRONIC RESOURCE MANAGEMENT SOLUTIONS [9]

TDNet ERM Solutions are the proprietary product of TDNetInc., developed in 2000. It offers e-resource access as well as management (ERAM) solutions for communities like academic, corporate, government, and others.

4.3.1 Features

- Flexibility and customization of management and A-to-Z holdings.
- Scalable, multilevel customization and personalization.
- Federated searching for both internal and external e-resources.
- Classification-based analysis.
- Availability of eBook Manager.
- Generates statistics on per product, per provider, per time slot, etc.

4.3.2 Standards and Compatibility

The standards that run compatible with TDNET ERM solutions are COUNTER, Delimited, Excel and Text format support, Full-text resolver, MARC, NISO, ONIX, OpenURL, SOH (Serial Online Holdings), SUSHI, and XML.

4.3.3 Functions and Modules

It provides unique functions such as single point of maintenance, e-book management, public display functions, collection evaluation, authentication management, reporting, etc. It manages access permissions via IP/access details/access notes/support specific access solutions (Athens). Access can be differentiated by user identity, e.g., when belonging to a predefined group.

4.4 ALMA ELECTRONIC RESOURCE MANAGEMENT [10]

A commercial software product, the first Alma ERM was released in 2012 by Ex Libris. Ex Libris has added new features and enhancements around most of Alma's workflows and integration with Primo—the Ex Libris discovery solution. Alma is the perfect solution that all libraries need as the focal point of learning and research in various institutions. It has been designed to handle all e-resource types and support library collaboration, so as to optimize user experience, as well as providing collection through rich analytics. Alma has been designed to ensure that the entire collection can be managed through a single interface that can continue to serve students, instructors, and researchers with a collection optimized for their needs. In addition, Alma fully supports the collaboration that is crucial for institutions in the modern academic environment, with built-in support for different levels of consortium arrangements. In the first release of Alma, the feature descriptions for relative components are Acquisitions, Metadata, Fulfillment, Primo Integration, SaaS, and Security.

4.4.1 Features

- Eliminates the need to work to synchronize data across systems.
- Comprehensive analytics designed for the whole collection.
- Highlights the differentiators of a library's collection.
- Demand-driven collection development increases collection usage.
- Integrated data services enable streamlined ordering and cataloguing.
- Hybrid shared/local data environment ensures that local needs are supported.
- Non-MARC metadata schemas support description of an array of resources.
- Optimizing resource utilization by highlighting available resources.

- User-friendly patron interactions.
- Precision in tracking quality of service to patrons.
- Adherence to open standards and open APIs allows libraries to extend the system.
- Streamlining integrations via industry standard open interfaces.
- Advanced customization options using open interfaces.
- No management of local hardware, clients, or upgrades.
- Reduces the technical expertise required for basic management activities.
- Subscription model provides for more predictable budgeting.
- Deployed as a cloud-based solution, Alma allows libraries to eliminate hardware and maintenance investments. The entire Alma interface is served via a web browser. In addition to removing the need to manage and maintain local servers, Alma frees system administration staff from the need to install and maintain clients on local PCs.

4.4.2 Standards and Compatibility

Alma is an open architecture and with support for industry standards such as SIP2, EDI, OAI-PMH, COUNTER 4, SUSHI, NISO Circ (NCIP 2), RDA—as MARC encoded fields, MARC21, Dublin Core, MARCXML, Z39.50, ISO2709 is supported in its MARC21/UNIMARC versions, RFID—supported as part of our development roadmap, KBART—we support the export and import of KBART data, ONIX—we support the import of ONIX based license data, AACR2—is supported in its MARC21 version, DCRM(B)—it is possible to catalogue all necessary characters for DCRM(B) in Alma.

4.4.3 Functions and Modules

Users can access e-resources via an A-to-Z list, library portals, library OPAC, or link servers. It provides functionality such as cataloguing, acquisitions, resource management, circulation, and administration.

4.5 WEB-SHARE LICENSE MANAGER [11]

Web-share License Manager was developed by OCLC. It helps manage divergent e-content workflows and has everything in one place, so that time and money can be saved, thereby making collection development easier.

4.5.1 Features

- A unique ERM solution that consolidates the management of link resolution with the vendor, manages subscriptions, licenses and centralized acquisition.
- Acts as a single platform to access all library e-resources.
- Provides analytics that help make informed library management decisions. It is compliant with COUNTER to generate statistics.
- It takes care of other aspects of the job like evaluation of trial subscriptions, negotiation of licenses with content providers, registration and configuration of access to e-resources, support for EZproxy.

4.5.2 Standards and Compatibility

The standards compatible with Web-share License Manager are COUNTER, Ezproxy, OCLC MARC Format, Open URL link resolver, Z39.50 search, and Retrieval Protocol.

4.5.3 Function and Modules

The modules of Web-share License Manager are metadata, acquisitions, licenses, circulation, admin, and help. It is compatible with OpenURL link resolver, and manages interlibrary loan, course reserves, and archival material of e-resources. Other functions such as remote access, A-to-Z list, postcancelation access, citation finder tool for articles, copying and sharing, and API Web Service for the WorldCat knowledge base give benefits to users.

4.6 THE SEMPER TOOL DIGITAL LIBRARY SUITE [12]

The Semper Tool Digital Library Suite is an open source ERM software developed by SemperTool and can be installed by the system LAMP (Linux, Apache, MySQL, Perl). SMDB uses "webUtil" for web forms and templates.

4.6.1 Features

- The Resource Management System (RMS) manages all subscriptions, licenses, and resources. It has a fully customizable knowledge base that can be customized as per the institution's specific holdings.
- The A-to-Z products and resources generate alphabetical listings of individual products (databases) and all resources (e-journals, e-books, etc.).

These lists can be exported and easily made available on library websites.

- Link resolver determines the exact availability of content, based on the specific entitlements of the library with the GetMeThere (GMT) OpenURL-based link resolver. It enables librarians and users to have accurate information regarding the availability of e-resources in the library.
- The system can automatically generate, compile, and store COUNTER compliant usage reports for all electronic resources through the SUSHI client.
- It delivers powerful search and discovery functionality to end-users with the LibHub central index search system. It enables users to efficiently browse and search across all library resources (electronic and physical), and locate relevant information through a single, intuitive, and effective search interface.
- It automatically generates a range of reports for a complete overview of licensing and expenditure. This allows effective management of licensing contacts, renewals, cancelations, and library finances.

4.6.2 Standards and Compatibility

SMDB supports standards such as SUSHI, GetMeThere (GMT) OpenURL-based link resolver.

4.6.3 Functions and Modules

The functions and modules are products, providers, resources, publishers, subjects, organizations, reports, users, and setup. In addition to this it includes managing product and resources types, and also manages agents and currencies.

4.7 CENTRALIZED ONLINE RESOURCES ACQUISITION AND LICENSING [13]

Centralized Online Resources Acquisition and Licensing (CORAL) is an open source ERMS available on GitHub and developed by the University of Notre Dame's Hesburgh Libraries, released in the year 2010. It runs on PHP 5, MySQL 5, and webserver. CORAL has facilities for the management of e-resource workflow, starting from the overall acquisition process to ongoing support and maintenance.

4.7.1 Features

- "Resources" is the most recent addition to the CORAL suite, and it assists in the management of the complete e-resource workflow. It is highly customizable through an administrative front end and has robust search features, as well as the new ability to export search results into excel. It supports resources including subscription alert e-mails, and customizable "notes" fields. It has the ability to upload attachments and also keep track of contact information. If the licensing module is used, an individual resource can be linked to a specific license for quick access. Parent/child relationships can be set up with any resources for increased accessibility.

- Licensing features provide a way to store and access digital copies of current and expired license agreements and related documents, as well as associated agreement metadata. It helps make library license agreements more accessible to personnel through selected searchable metadata fields, and assists institutions in tracking specific pieces of information included in legal agreements. The license clauses are customized through the administrative front end. They rope in signature tracking, the ability to associate organizations and consortia, as well as the ability to upload any additional attachments. Licensing has an add-on for delivering up the license terms within the context of accessing a specific resource. The Licensing Terms Tool add-on works by querying either the SFX or SerialsSolutions OpenURL resolver API to obtain the available resource holdings, and then queries the licensing module for the governing license terms. Interlibrary loan staff, e.g., will find this easy-to-use add-on invaluable in identifying the interlibrary rights governing electronic journals.

- Organization modules store and manage names, contacts, and account information for the many publishers, providers, and vendors that libraries interact with on a daily basis, all within a single location. It hires a robust administrative front end to control drop down values—e.g., contact roles or organizational roles.

- At present, Usage Statistics supports JR1 and JR1a COUNTER reports, or any noncounter reports edited into a counter-like format. Management of the statistics is made available by both publisher and platform. Each platform or provider can be linked to a specific organization in the Organizations module, which will in turn import all associated account information. This allows organizations to be a single point of entry for all administrative account data. In the case of any publisher-reported errors, or if the need arises to import statistics for any reason, then individual months of data can be removed by the publisher platform. Usage statistics can also check for "outlier" statistics in all imported data, and can flag the title/month of the suspicious data. This outlier use is flagged both within the user interface and within exported reports using color coding for easy identification. Usage Statistics Reports is a front end to the Usage Statistics database designed to be used by staff and collection managers for running their own reports.

- The management module stores documents, such as policies, processes, and procedures, related to the overall management of e-resources. Each document can be assigned a type and can be stored in a separate record. Related documents can also be assigned a category so that they can be grouped together. When a new version of a document is created, the previous version is archived. This way the history of a document can be preserved by making notes and assigning to a specific document version.

4.7.2 Standards and Compatibility

CORAL is compatible with the standards such as LDAP (lightweight directory access protocol), MySQL, ONIX-PL, JR1, and JR1a COUNTER.

4.7.3 Functions and Modules

It has four major modules, Resource, Licensing, Organizations, Usage and Management.

4.8 360 RESOURCE MANAGER [14]

Serials Solutions 360 Resource Manager is a proprietary ERM software developed in 2005. It is an e-resource knowledge based system which provides consistent and accurate access, and streamlined management of e-resources.

4.8.1 Features

- The consortium edition increases the value of membership by managing and sharing consortium purchase, inheritance, and member details through a streamlined interface that creates more efficient data management and discovery.

- Reporting increases efficiency, saves money, and simplifies e-resource management, with standardized reports including specialized reports and unique identifiers to maximize value and foster interoperability.
- Import acquisitions, cost, and contact information from ILS, spreadsheets, and other systems for fast, efficient, and accurate updating.
- Collection management associates costs and resources with collections that libraries define to meet their needs.
- Track cost and payment in an easy-to-use format and enjoy associated reporting functionality. Cost-per-user reporting is available when combined with 360 counter.
- It can integrate with discovery service, link resolver, and A-to-Z list
- It can manage local, vendor, and consortia contacts.
- Resource notes manager manages track acquisition notes, outage reports, license breaches, historical information, and more.
- Maintain details about resource licenses and terms of use, and expose that information through discovery services.
- Easily customize the administrative interface to reflect local needs and enhance workflow.
- Track the status of all e-resources as they move through the e-resource lifecycle.
- Manage renewal dates, user logins, and other valuable administrative data.
- Set alerts for license renewals and status changes.
- Manage access and collection for vendors' usage statistics.
- Overlap analysis allows you to identify overlapping coverage using actual coverage dates.
- Create permission-based views and access to information for a wide variety of staff and needs.
- Generate usage statistics and count how often users use journals and databases.

4.8.2 Standards and Compatibility

The standards compatible with 360 Resource Manager are COUNTER and SUSHI, CrossRef DOI Linking, MARC, NISO, OAI-PMH, ONIX SRU/SRW, OpenURL, SOAP, SOH, and XML.

4.8.3 Functions and Modules

It provides holdings, bibliographic metadata, cost data, acquisition information, licensing information, and other such details to users to ensure easy access.

4.9 GOLD RUSH [15]

Gold Rush was originally developed in 2001 by the Colorado Alliance of Research Libraries to help its member libraries organize their e-resources. At this time, ERMs were not available in the commercial market place. In 2003 Alliance started to offer Gold Rush to libraries that existed outside the consortium. By this time, all libraries in the entire nation have licensed Gold Rush. Today, Gold Rush continues to be a popular ERM as it has been continually upgraded. It is also cost-effective and offers strong customer support. Gold Rush provides open access journals that can be selected and added to local holdings at no additional cost.

4.9.1 Features

- It is hosted in a server that is centrally located and therefore requires no local server. It can be integrated within any library system and included within a library website.
- It allows libraries to create and track information about subscriptions for e-resources such as cost, terms and conditions, and contacts. This will make it easier for libraries to customize templates without any programmer intervention to make the system tailor-made for local needs.
- OpenURL link resolution provides seamless access to e-resources starting from library catalogues and other direct links to articles.
- The decision support module allows library staff to compare title lists from over 1500 aggregators, publishers, and indexing/abstracting services that have been loaded. It provides scope for comparison of the content available within packages, even if the library does not subscribe to them. This is especially helpful for collection development, library administration, and reference staff who are trying to make tough decisions on what products to be purchased or canceled.
- In general, all reports are generated in real-time over the web and viewed on most standard browsers or downloaded into Microsoft

Excel. Title lists are also updated on a regular basis in order to provide the latest and best information possible.

- It covers both full-texts as well as indexed-only titles.
- It monitors contracts, pricing, and the renewal process. It creates customized reports.
- It has OpenURL link resolver compliance for NISO 1.0 and 0.1 standards. Control style sheets and results page templates as per clients needs.
- Public search interface offers A-to-Z browsing, and full title, keyword, and ISSN searching.
- It controls its own style sheets which result in page templates. It can also create a customized interface.

4.9.2 Standards and Compatibility

Standards compatible in Gold Rush are OpenURL link resolver, with full compliance for NISO 1.0 and 0.1 standards, SOAP Protocol, Support Excel format, SUSHI, and XML.

4.9.3 Functions and Modules

Modules available in Gold Rush ERMS are Reports, Holdings, Subscriptions, Cataloguing, and Settings.

4.10 EBSCONET ELECTRONIC RESOURCE MANAGEMENT ESSENTIALS [16]

EBSCONET ERM Essentials were developed by EBSCO in 2010. It is an e-resource management tool that maintains approximately 100 highly customizable data fields for e-journal and e-package orders.

4.10.1 Features

- Manages e-journals and e-packages with single-point access.
- It facilitates the management of e-resource development decisions through trials, evaluations, licensing management, orders, and renewals.
- Streamlines e-resource management processes by setting status, creating reminders, and assigning tasks.
- Generates different types of reports.

4.10.2 Standards and Compatibility

EBSCONET ERM Essentials are compatible with standards such as ANSI/NISO, CORE (Cost of Resource Exchange), HTML Format, MARC, ONIX, OpenURL link resolver, Support Excel format, support proxy, and XML.

4.10.3 Functions and Modules

Modules available in this ERM Essentials are My collection, Renewal, Upload, Reminders, Tasks, Options, and Reports.

4.11 E-RESOURCE CENTRAL [17]

E-resource Central is an e-resource management solution for libraries developed in 2011 by SirsiDynix. It bridges the gap between content providers and users, and enables libraries to manage and deliver e-resources seamlessly and cost-effectively.

4.11.1 Features

- It is a single-user interface providing access to all library e-resources.
- It manages licensing and access rights, maintains MARC records and metadata, integrates e-resource usage into circulation reports, and manages e-content acquisition and creation.
- Tools used for the access of e-resources and their download process simplify the work of the end-user.

4.11.2 Standards and Compatibility

Standards compatible with eResource central are MARC, ONIX, and XML.

Electronic Resource Management Systems are another tool that address the complexity of data for the purpose of managing e-resources. This software tries to integrate all components of ERM such as knowledge base, subscription and purchase of e-journals, e-books, databases, budget, licensing, administration, reports, access control, and management within a single body. Libraries facing difficulties in managing e-resources with all the various steps and procedures required should opt for the implementation of ERMS. Comparisons and evaluation of the standards, features, and functions used in the ERM software designed especially for managing e-resources have been represented in this chapter. Based on this comparison, libraries/librarians can take this as a ready reference to match their needs, using facilities offered by ERMS. This will be a very handy tool in making the right choice and deciding upon the selection of ERMS for efficient management of e-resources.

REFERENCES

[1] E. McCracken, Description of and access to electronic resources (ER): transitioning into the digital age, Collect. Manage. 32 (3—4) (2007) 259—275.

[2] M. Breeding, Helping you buy: electronic resource management systems, Comput. Libraries 28 (7) (2008). Retrieved April 1, 2014, from http://www.librarytechnology.org/ltg-displaytext.pl?RC=13437.

[3] T.A. Fons, T.D. Jewell, Envisioning the future of ERM systems, Serials Librarians 52 (1—2) (2007) 151—166. Retrieved May 09, 2015, from http://atlas.tk.informatik.tudarmstadt.de/Publications/1999/electronic.pdf.

[4] T.D. Jewell, I. Anderson, A. Chandler, S.E. Farb, K. Parker, N.D. Robertson, Electronic Resource Management. The Report of the DLF Initiative, Digital Library Federation, Washington, DC, 2004. Retrieved July 18, 2015, from http://www.diglib.org/pubs/dlf102.

[5] T. Jewell, DLF Electronic Resource Management Initiative, Phase II: Final Report, Digital Library Federation and Council on Library and Information Resources, Washington, DC, 2008. Retrieved July 17, 2013, from http://old.diglib.org/standards/ERMI2_Final_Report_20081230.pdf.

[6] T. Carpenter, B. McQuillan, O. Pesch, The Three S's of Electronic Resource Management: Systems, Standards, and Subscriptions. NISO Webinars, 2011. Retrieved May 09, 2013, from http://www.niso.org/news/events/2011/nisowebinars/erm.

[7] M. Collins, J.E. Grogg, At ERMS length: evaluating electronicresource management systems, Library J. 136 (4) (2011) 22—28. Retrieved April 1, 2013, from http://www.libraryjournal.com/lj/ljinprintspecialty/889092-480/building_abetter_erms.html.csp.

[8] Innovative ERM, http://www.iii.com/products/electronic_resource.shtml.

[9] TDNet ERM Solutions, http://www.tdnet.io/.

[10] Alma ERM, http://www.exlibrisgroup.com/category/AlmaOverview.

[11] Web-share License Manager, https://www.oclc.org/license-manager.en.html.

[12] The Semper Tool Digital Library Suite (DLS), http://www.sempertool.dk/.

[13] CORAL, http://coral-erm.org/.

[14] 360 ResourceManager, http://www.proquest.com/products-services/360-Resource-Manager.html.

[15] Rush G., https://www.coalliance.org/software/gold-rush.

[16] EBSCONET' ERM Essentials, http://www2.ebsco.com/hi-in/ProductsServices/ERM/Pages/ERMInfo.aspx.

[17] E-Resource Central, http://www.sirsidynix.com/products/eresource-central.

CHAPTER 5

Standards, Compatibility, and Best Practices for Electronic Resource Management

To manage all the steps in the lifecycle of e-resources, Electronic Resource Management System (ERMS) should be interoperated with an existing Library Management System (LMS), as well as with other applications present there. The use of standards is inevitable in the case of any ERMS. The specifications published by the Digital Library Federation's (DLF) Electronic Resource Management Initiative (ERMI) (DLF-ERMI www.diglib.org/standards/dlf-erm02.htm) in 2004 have become the de facto standard for the development of ERMS [1]. Although ERM software leverages and expands earlier standards work (MARC, Onix for Serials, openURL, metasearch, etc.), the DLF ERMI specification is considered the underlying guide to cater to the functional requirements and data elements of modern ERMS. In the second phase is the group ERMII; a major objective here is to develop standards for the collection of license information and usage statistics, which would help reduce the administrative costs of both data sets. A few recent attempts such as the Standardized Usage Statistics Harvesting Initiative (SUSHI) and the License Expression Work Group, are defining new standards and protocols to address the new ERM issue.

The popular standards for licensing information include the Online Information Exchange (ONIX) for Publications Licenses (ONIX-PL) that created encoded exchange of licensing terms, NISO's License Expression Working Group that mapped the license syntax between ERMI and ONIX, and NISO's Shared E-Resources Understanding (SERU) that provided guidelines for those who want to forego negotiated licenses. In order to track the usage of e-resources, there has been a development in the Counting Online Usage of Networked Electronic Resources (COUNTER) codes of practice which has established a standard for what is counted and how. The success of COUNTER resulted

Digital Disruption and Electronic Resource Management in Libraries.
DOI: http://dx.doi.org/10.1016/B978-0-08-102045-6.00005-4

in the formation of NISO's SUSHI, a protocol devised to automate the harvesting of COUNTER data. Another significant new capability introduced with e-resources was OpenURL linking. OpenURL evolved into a formal standard (ANSI/NISO Z39.88) and generated another project, the NISO/UKSG Knowledge Base and Related Tools (KBART) initiative. What they did was issue their recommended practices so as to improve the quality of OpenURL knowledge bases along with their metadata. Another NISO project, Improving OpenURLs Through Analytics (IOTA), is looking at how to measure the quality of this metadata. Systems-related standards efforts for ERM include NISO's Cost of Resource Exchange (CORE) project to develop a protocol for exchanging finances between an integrated library system (ILS) and an ERM, and a project to develop best practices for single sign-on authentication so users do not have to log in over and over. Some of these projects have had tremendous success and are being rapidly adopted in the community. SUSHI and SERU are two examples whose success points to the underlying reasons why standards are adopted, generally. The reason behind SUSHI's success is the gathering of usage data from not just dozens, but hundreds of content suppliers. For SERU it was the effort to negotiate licenses which becomes completely unsaleable when the number of licenses reaches a few dozen [2].

The lifecycle of ERM complies with some standards which are represented in Figs. 5.1−5.5.

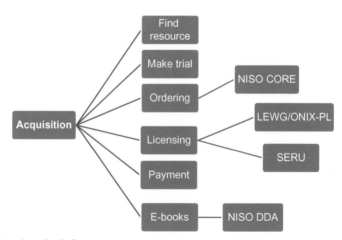

Figure 5.1 Standards for acquisition management.

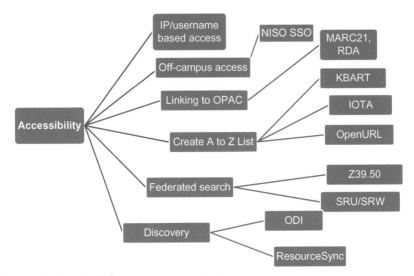

Figure 5.2 Standards for access management.

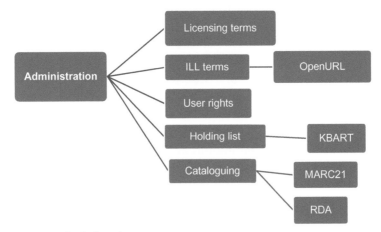

Figure 5.3 Standards for administration management.

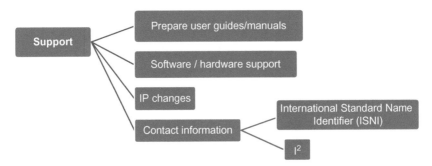

Figure 5.4 Standards for support management.

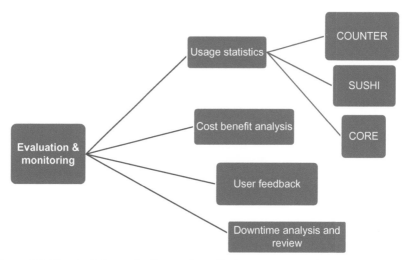

Figure 5.5 Standards for evaluation and monitoring management.

The details of ERM related standards, best practices, and related initiatives are also represented in Table 5.1 [3].

As mentioned in Table 5.1, ERM standards focus basically on five general categories, including: (1) link resolvers and knowledge bases; (2) the work, its manifestations, and access points; (3) integration of usage and cost-related data; (4) coding license terms and defining consensus; and (5) data exchange using institutional identifiers (I^2). The descriptions of each standard follow.

5.1 LINK RESOLVERS AND KNOWLEDGE BASES

Though the link resolvers and knowledge bases have completely different diverse functions, they perform a similar genre of function in connecting users with content during the linking processes. In order to lead the user from a citation source to the full-text target, the link resolver relies on the accuracy of the data found in the library's holding knowledge base, i.e., the list of e-resources.

5.1.1 OpenURL

An OpenURL linkage refers to electronic information delivery. An OpenURL framework application is a networked service environment in which packages of information are transported over a network. These packages generally comprise of descriptions of one referenced source.

Table 5.1 Electronic resource management related standards, best practices, and related initiatives

Acronym	Name	Admin body	Synopsis	Standard	Best practice	For more information
1. Link resolvers and knowledge bases						
1.1 Open URL	Open Uniform Resource Locator (URL)	OCLC (under NISO)	A URL that includes a context-sensitive description of a referenced resource and a service request	X		http://www.oclc.org/research/activities/openurl.html
1.2 KBART	Knowledge Bases and Related Tools	NISO/UKSG	Aimed at effecting smoother interaction between members of the knowledge base supply chain		X	http://www.niso.org/workrooms/kbart
1.3 IOTA	Improving OpenURLs Through Analytics	NISO	Initiative to investigate the feasibility of creating industry-wide, transparent, and scalable metrics for evaluating and comparing the quality of OpenURL implementations across content providers			http://www.niso.org/workrooms/openurlquality http://openurlquality.niso.org/
2. The work, its manifestations, and access points						
2.1 DOI	Digital Object Identifier System	Intl DOI Foundation	System for persistent identification of content on digital networks	X		http://www.doi.org/
2.2 MARC21	Machine Readable Catalogue	Library of Congress	Standards for representation and communication of bibliographic and related information in machine-readable form	X		http://www.loc.gov/marc/

(Continued)

Table 5.1 (Continued)

Acronym	Name	Admin body	Synopsis	Standard	Best practice	For more information
2.3 ONIX for Serials	Online Information eXchange for Serials	EDItEUR	A family of XML formats for communicating information about serial products and subscription information	X		http://www.editeur.org/17/ONIX-for-Serials/
2.3.1 SOH	ONIX serial Serials Online Holdings	EDItEUR	A format for communicating serials holdings or coverage information	X		http://www.editeur.org/120/SOH/
2.3.2 SPS	ONIX Serials Products and Subscriptions	EDItEUR	A format for communicating information about serials subscription products	X		http://www.editeur.org/121/SPS/
2.3.3 SRN	ONIX Serials Release Notification	EDItEUR	A format for communicating information about the publication or availability of serials releases	X		http://www.editeur.org/122/SRN
2.4 ONIX for Books	ONIX for Books	EDItEUR	An XML format for representing and communicating book industry product information in electronic form	X		http://www.editeur.org/83/Overview/
2.5 PIE-J	Presentation and Identification of E-journals	NISO	Guidance in the areas of e-journal title presentation and bibliographic history, accurate use of ISSN, and citation practice		Forthcoming	http://www.niso.org/workrooms/piej

2.6 TRANSFER	Transfer Code of Practice	UKSG	Guidelines for transfer of journals from publisher to publisher ensure that journal content remains easily accessible	X		http://www.uksg.org/transfer
2.7 ISTC	International Standard Text Code	Intl ISTC Agency	A numbering system to enable unique identification of textual works		X	http://www.istc-international.org/html/
2.8 ISBN	International Standard Book Number	Intl ISBN Agency	Unique product identifier for ordering, listing, sales records, and stock control of monographic publications		X	http://www.isbn-international.org/
2.9 ISSN-L	Linking ISSN	ISSN Intl Centre	An ISSN that groups different media versions of a continuing resource		X	http://www.issn.org/2-22637-What-is-an-ISSN-L.php
3. Integration of usage and cost-related data						
3.1 CORE	Cost of Resource Exchange	NISO	Facilitates transfer of cost and related financial information from an ILS to an ERMS		X	http://www.niso.org/workrooms/core
3.2 COUNTER	Counting Online Usage of Networked Electronic Resources	COUNTER Online Metrics	Sets standards to facilitate consistent recording and reporting of online usage statistics		X	http://www.projectcounter.org/
3.3 SUSHI	Standardized Usage Harvesting Initiative	NISO	Defines an automated request and response model for the harvesting of e-resource usage statistics		X	http://www.niso.org/workrooms/sushi

(*Continued*)

Table 5.1 (Continued)

Acronym	Name	Admin body	Synopsis	Standard	Best practice	For more information
4. Coding license terms and defining consensus						
4.1 OLT	ONIX for Licensing Terms	EDItEUR	Family of messaging formats for communication of rights information	X		http://www.editeur.org/85/Overview/
4.1.1 ONIX-PL	ONIX for Publication Licenses	EDItEUR	XML formats for communication of license terms under which libraries and other institutions use digital resources	X		http://www.editeur.org/21/ONIX-PL/
4.1.2 ONIX for RROs	ONIX for Reproduction Rights Organizations	EDItEUR	XML formats for facilitating communication by collective management organizations and the publishers and authors with whom they work	X		http://www.editeur.org/23/ONIX-for-RROs/
4.2 SERU	Shared Electronic Resource Understanding	NISO	Set of statements of common understanding for subscribing to electronic resources	X		http://www.niso.org/workrooms/seru
5. Data exchange using institutional identifiers						
5.1 i²	Institutional Identifiers	NISO	Provides guidelines for using the International Standard Name Identifier (ISNI) as an institutional identifier for library and publishing environments		Forth-coming	http://www.niso.org/workrooms/i2

5.2 WorldCat Registry	WorldCat® Registry	OCLC	Web-based directory for libraries and library consortia to use as an authoritative single source for information that defines institutional identity, services, relationships, contracts, and other key data often shared with third parties		http://www.worldcat.org/registry/Institutions
5.3 Shibboleth	Shibboleth® System	Internet2 Middleware Initiative	A standards-based, open source software package for web single sign-on across or within organizational boundaries	X	http://www.internet2.edu/shibboleth
5.4 vCard	vCard (originally Versit Card)	Internet Mail Consortium	Schema for electronic business cards	X	http://www.imc.org/pdi/vcardoverview.html

These packages are then transported with the intention of obtaining a context-sensitive service that pertains to the reference sources. It checks the metadata of a citation from an abstracting and indexing resource against the library's knowledge base holding, and based on these holdings retrieves and displays the appropriate copy for that citation from another resource that has the desired full-text.

5.1.2 Knowledge Bases and Related Tools

This explores data problems within the OpenURL supply chain. When all is working well, link resolver helps library users connect to electronic resources provided by their respective institutions. The data that drives such a tool is stored in a knowledge base. The quality of data fed into the knowledge base depends on the data that content providers, i.e., publishers and aggregators, etc., send to the knowledge base developer. Because there is no standard format for such data, knowledge developers have to work with caution and perception while converting title lists from various providers to a single format. This may make error checking a difficult task to perform. For ERM, KBART offers an improvement in OpenURL linking, and improvement in the accuracy and timeliness of metadata in the ERM system.

5.1.3 Improving OpenURLs Through Analytics

This measures the quality of the source of the OpenURL links generated by content providers. It makes use of log files from various institutions and vendors to analyze element frequencies and patterns contained within the OpenURL strings. The reports that are generated from log files analyses inform direct Open URL providers about the places that require improvement, so that the maximum number of OpenURL requests resolve to offer correct records.

5.2 THE WORK, ITS MANIFESTATIONS, AND ACCESS POINTS

This category comes under the standard of identifying resources (articles or other entities of interest).

5.2.1 Digital Object Identifier System

The purpose of Digital Object Identifier (DOI) is to persistently identify digital objects across the internet. The system incorporates an identifier syntax, a resolution component, appropriate metadata, and a formal structure to support the standard.

5.2.2 Machine Readable Catalogue (MARC21)

This standard provides the systemic capability of reading and transmitting bibliographic data. It also serves as the foundation for online library catalogues.

5.2.3 Online Information Exchange for Serials

This is basically a family of XML formats that communicate information about serial products and subscription information, using the design principles and many of the elements defined in ONIX for books.

5.2.4 Serials Online Holdings

The serials online holdings (SOH) messages are used for communicating information about the holdings or coverage of online serial resources from a party that holds or supplies the resources to a party that needs this information in its system. The messages include details of serial versions, formats available, hosted collections in which the serial version are found, and coverage information for each serial version. The SOH coverage information includes the extent of coverage of each resource (date ranges, volume/issue ranges, or both) along with details of any applicable embargo.

5.2.5 Serials Products and Subscriptions

The serials products and subscriptions (SPS) format defines a family of messages used for transmitting information about serial subscription products, with or without price information, and with or without subscription information relating to a particular subscriber.

5.2.6 Serials Release Notification

The serials release notification (SRN) format defines a family of messages that have been designed to support information exchanges about planned or confirmed publications, or the electronic availability of one or more serial releases.

The ONIX for serials message formats generally support much more granular value definitions for specific elements, and this greater granularity could prove useful in the ERM environment.

5.2.7 Transfer

The Transfer Code of Practice relates to the needs of the scholarly journal community, that have been put forward by them. It generally comprises of a string of guidelines to help publishers determine the easy accessibility of the information to users, as well as librarians, whenever there is a transfer between the parties. This is done to ensure that the transfer process happens with minimum disruption. When journals change ownership, many critical issues can arise. They include continuity of access during a transfer, and whether perpetual ongoing access to archives is retained in journal sale agreements. This has resulted in frustration for end users and librarians, as key e-journals became temporarily or even permanently unavailable despite license terms. Publishers who have endorsed the Transfer Code of Practice agree to best practice guidelines and responsibilities that ensure that the content present within the journals remains easily accessible to users, even if ownership changes. When publishers endorse transfer, libraries and end users benefit with minimal disruption in service. For ERM, tracking and managing the movement of titles become less problematic.

5.3 INTEGRATION OF USAGE AND COST-RELATED DATA

Librarians generally bear a long-standing interest in having comparable usage statistics. This facilitates the process of getting information which helps to assess cost and expenditure. The initiatives described are all intended to address these issues in one way or another.

5.3.1 Cost of Resource Exchange

CORE protocols are designed to facilitate the transfer of cost and related financial information from an ILS acquisition module (the source) to an ERMS (the requestor). The population of ERMS financial data from an ILS acquisition system makes cost-per-click and other cost-related reports in the ERMS all the more possible.

5.3.2 Counting Online Usage of Networked Electronic Resources (COUNTER)

The COUNTER is a set standard to acquire usage reports of online e-resources.

5.3.3 Standardized Usage Statistics Harvesting Initiative

The SUSHI protocol defines a request and response model for the automated harvesting of usage statistics of e-resources through a web services framework. It replaces the difficulty of manual downloading and collecting of usage statistics by libraries.

5.4 CODING LICENSE TERMS AND DEFINING CONSENSUS

Here, two standards help in dealing with the prevalence of licenses and licensing within the digital and ERM environment, which grew out of perceived needs by information creators and providers for protection not offered under the fair use provision of copyright law.

5.4.1 Online Information Exchange for Publication Licenses (ONIX-PL)

ONIX-PL is specialized to handle the licenses under which libraries and other institutions use digital resources, particularly but not exclusively for e-journals.

5.4.2 Shared Electronic Resource Understanding

A SERU describes common understandings related to e-resource subscriptions. It addresses issues of special relevance to e-books, such as perpetual access and numbers of pages that can be downloaded or printed. It thus shows the promise of streamlining the acquisition as well as licensing of e-resources, all the while emphasizing lower overheads and quicker access for the end user.

5.5 DATA EXCHANGE USING INSTITUTIONAL IDENTIFIERS

Another set of long-standing problems shared by the information providers and libraries, the ERM environment relates to readily identifying the parties involved and associating contact demography, IP range, and other administrative information with them.

5.5.1 Institutional Identifier

I^2 supports the exchange of information within the information supply chain, which includes publishers, vendors, consortia, and libraries. It is useful to ERMS.

5.5.2 WorldCat@Registry

This is an online public repository of data about individual libraries and consortia. Participating institutions receive an identifier, which vendors, content providers, or other libraries can use to quickly gain access to information such as administrative contacts and IP addresses. Links to the library's OpenURL servers, the online catalogue, and virtual reference service can be used to make the library's web services and its content easily accessible to online users. The WorldCat@Registry is maintained by the OCLC, which is in charge of distributing the data to open source services. These services also include its own Worldcat.org for maximizing the visibility of the participating institutions.

5.5.3 Shibboleth

This is an open source authentication software that provides single sign-on capabilities across an institution's web space. It uses SAML (Security Assertion Markup Language) metadata in order to exchange information between an identifier and a service provider.

5.5.4 vCard

The main purpose of vCard is the exchange of information about people and resources. For ERMS, this standard would be very useful for capturing and storing contact information for sales representatives, vendor executives, and library or consortia representatives.

There are a number of relevant standards and best practices that have been developed over the last several years. Now it is important to implement these standards in ERMS.

REFERENCES

[1] R. Kasprowski, Standards in electronic resource management, Bull. Am. Soc. Inf. Sci. Technol. 33 (6) (2007) 32–37.
[2] T. Carpenter, Standard columns, electronic resource management standardization: still a mixed bag, 2010. Retrieved March 30, 2015, from http://www.niso.org/apps/group_public/download.php/5258/.
[3] T. Jewell, J. Aipperspach, I. Anderson, D. England, R. Kasprowski, B. McQuillan, et al., Making Good on the Promise of ERM: A Standards and Best Practices Discussion Paper, NISO, Baltimore, 2012. Retrieved July 17, 2013, from http://www.niso.org/apps/group_public/download.php/7946.

CHAPTER 6

Electronic Resource Management Systems: Pros and Cons

6.1 BENEFITS OF ELECTRONIC RESOURCE MANAGEMENT

Electronic Resource Management Systems (ERMS) prove their usefulness for both the librarian and library users. Some of the benefits of implementing ERMS are as follows:

1. Effective and efficient management of digital collections workflow (lifecycle), i.e., starting from evaluation, selection, acquisition, renewal/review/cancelation and access to troubleshooting.
2. Keeping track of license agreements, and managing online subscriptions, coverage data, and A-to-Z holdings, etc.
3. One-stop Solution: ERMS facilitate viewing of all information related to particular e-resources without having to consult multiple files/spreadsheets.
4. An ERMS analyzes the usage statistics and cost-per-use, as well as licensing information. It also helps in examining particular e-resources without needing to consult many files or spreadsheets.
5. The system allows users to search multiple databases simultaneously and get combined results in a uniform format.
6. An ERMS offers a central system for monitoring the management of link resolutions with vendors, negotiation of licenses with content providers, evaluation of trial subscriptions, subscription management, centralized acquisition, budgeting, and ordering, etc.
7. An evaluation and monitoring module provides usage statistics, users' feedback, and downtime analysis which support the renewal/review/cancelation of e-resources.
8. Information alerts are provided through login pop-ups and e-mails, and remind the librarian to renew the license for the resources before they are terminated. In case there is a change of e-resources URL

Digital Disruption and Electronic Resource Management in Libraries.
DOI: http://dx.doi.org/10.1016/B978-0-08-102045-6.00006-6

and/or IP changes of an institution, notifications go from the content provider to the librarian. This alert service also offers different kinds of notifications to users, such as the addition of new resources to the library, downtime notification, if any, etc.

9. An ERMS enables searching of A-to-Z lists available in the library, by title, author and subject, etc., direct to the full-text article via the OpenURL resolving standard. This leads to the formation of a single interface for all different units of information in the e-resources life-cycle. For example, librarians will be able to see the purchase details, such as coverage, cost, subscription period, and usage statistics of e-resources. Library staff dealing with acquisitions and periodicals can also keep track of license agreements, pricing, discounts, and payment terms. Cataloguing staff can see subscription dates and also access methods. Reference and other public services staff can be acquainted with new e-resources, usage restrictions, and rights. With the easy availability of contact information, staff can contact the content provider/technical support for a solution to any technical problems, and can inform users of any information alerting service. Thus, ERMS helps in streamlining workflows and disseminates information, hence eradicating the necessity of reentering data again and again. As defined by Sadeh and Ellingsen [1], ERMS is a "central control tower."

10. An ERMS exercises administrative control and restricts the library staff from reading, updating, creating, or deleting the authorization of e-resource workflow. Staff within the library can limit their activities within the security restriction zone as defined by the administrator. An acquisition staff login can be limited to view only the acquisition area, and they do not have the right to control/monitor the access management. Similarly, interlibrary loan (ILL) staff can only view data related to ILL usage.

11. Library staff get the opportunity to learn new tools, technology, and standards by implementing ERMS in the library.

12. Implementing ERMS requires staff from different departments to work together closely. Thus, the interrelationship and work camaraderie between staff of various departments improves. It provides opportunities for all to have all the sections related to e-resource management fit together.

6.2 WEAKNESSES OF ELECTRONIC RESOURCE MANAGEMENT SYSTEMS

Though the benefits of ERMS mentioned above are great news for both librarians and users, there are also certain weaknesses/perils that need to be addressed to ensure smooth workflow:

1. The main weakness in the case of most ERMS lies in the diversity of the digital collection, which includes digital images, streaming video, sound files, etc. The volumes are huge and need to be dealt with by staff with expertise.
2. Implementation of an ERMS system leads to a huge additional cost, as most of the proprietary ERMS are expensive.
3. For the purpose of implementing ERMS, a group of highly skilled professionals with expertise and knowledge in the field are needed.
4. The redundancy rate is very high in the case of personnel and technology after implementing ERMS.
5. Most of the functions are unique in all ERMS, but the paramount issue, i.e., basic structural features/modules are similar.
6. Integration of electronic resources in an ERMS is a taxing job which takes a long time.

6.3 SOME OF THE BEST PRACTICES IN ELECTRONIC RESOURCE MANAGEMENT SYSTEMS

Nowadays, speedy access to e-resources is crucial for users in any library. A library requires tools that are generally better than what the Integrated Library Management Systems offers to manage the diverse collection of e-resources. Librarians require details of the usage data as they tend to make escalating demands. Thus, many libraries are implementing ERMS to manage and administer e-resource products. Some of the institutions/university libraries that have already implemented ERMS are as follows:

1. University of California, USA: The library use Alma, from Ex Libris to manage e-resources.
2. California Institute of Technology, USA: The Caltech Library uses a series of spreadsheets, network drive files, and Google Drive, but have recently begun the process of migrating to a CORAL system that is hosted on a web server to manage e-resources.

3. University of Chicago, USA: To manage e-resources, the library use an Access database to track publications, and this database includes funding information, renewal dates, general scope of coverage, etc. In addition to this, SFX is used as a link resolver and to maintain an e-journal A-to-Z list.

4. Massachusetts Institute of Technology (MIT), USA: The library uses a FileMaker Pro database called VERA for managing e-resources. It was originally designed in the late 1990s. It has migrated through several versions of the FileMaker software, and updated fields, views, scripts, etc., to suit changing needs as the e-resource landscape has evolved over time.

5. Imperial College London, UK: The Central Library procured Ex Libris' Alma in July 2013 for managing e-resources, after previously adopting the Ex Libris Primo discovery solution. More recently, the library adopted the Leganto reading list solution in 2016, and integrated the Ex Libris UStat in 2015 to improve the Alma Analytics data analysis.

6. Duke University, USA: Duke Library does not currently utilize an ERM. In 2008−09 the library used Ex Libris' Verde briefly, but it could not meet the library's needs. However, they are tentatively waiting for FOLIO to be completed, which is stated to be a complete Library Service Platform that will include an ERM.

7. National University of Singapore, Singapore: The library is using the ERM module in Sierra from Innovative Interface Inc. Initially the library implemented Innopac for the Chinese Library in 1995, and then migrated the rest of the libraries in 1996−97. Then, it upgraded to Millennium in 2000 and moved to Sierra in December 2013. The library started using ERM in 2007.

8. Karolinska Institutet, Stockholm: The library used Alma from Ex Libris for ERM, and went live on June 4, 2015.

9. University of Washington, USA: The library started using the Ex Libris product, Alma, to manage e-resources in 2013.

10. New York University, USA: The library is not using an ERM system currently. However, they used the Innovative Interface Inc. (III) ERM as a stand-alone system (not integrated with Ex Libris's ILS) for a couple of years, but stopped using it about 5 years ago. Now the library uses a combination of systems and spreadsheets. To keep track of administrative information and contacts, the library use Serials Solutions, for financial information the library use Ex Libris'

Aleph, and for title lists it is used in a variety of ways. The library is in the midst of a project to track licensing in a more rational and shareable way.

11. University of Hong Kong, Hong Kong: At present, the library is using an in-house ERMS developed to manage their e-resources. However, they will move to Ex Libris' Alma in 2017.

12. Tsinghua University, China: The library have used SFX from Ex Libris to manage e-journals since 2005. In 2012, the library implemented Primo, supported by Ex Libris, for discovery service.

13. University of Edinburgh, UK: Since 2015 the library has used Ex Libris' Alma and Primo for efficient e-resource management, improved analytics, and a single search interface for users.

14. The University of Amsterdam, Netherlands: The library has a home-grown ERM system using applications such as Access database, Excel spreadsheets, and e-mail files.

15. University of Notre Dame Hesburgh, USA: The Hesburgh Library implemented the CORAL ERM system to manage e-resources in 2012. For copyright issues, the library use SIPX.

16. Hong Kong University of Science and Technology (KHUST), Hong Kong: The HKUST Library adopted an ERM system in 2005. It is one of the modules of ILS, Millennium, from Innovative Interfaces, Inc. The major features for managing e-resources in this system are resource, license, and contact.

17. University of California, Berkeley, USA: The library does not use a commercial ERM system. The library uses a series of internal spreadsheets to manage their e-resources.

18. University of Texas, Austin, USA: Currently the library uses Intota as an ERMS. The library migrated to Intota from 360 Resource Manager in March of 2016.

19. University of Oxford, Bodleian Libraries, UK: The libraries have used Knowledge Base (KB) + for managing e-resources since 2013.

20. Stanford University, California, USA: The library use CORAL (only the licensing module) and JIRA for workflow management. The library implemented CORAL in 2012, and JIRA in 2008.

21. Universitätsbibliothek der Humboldt-Universität zu Berlin, Germany: The library will be using Alma from Ex Libris in 2017 for managing their e-resources.

22. Cambridge University, UK: The library is using Alma from Ex Libris for ERM.

23. North Carolina State University, USA: The library currently uses E-Matrix, a locally developed ERM system, which was introduced in 2005. The library has also used CORAL to supplement E-Matrix since 2012.

6.4 TRAINING/EDUCATION IN ELECTRONIC RESOURCE MANAGEMENT

To manage e-resources through ERMS, it is essential to provide training and education to both LIS staff and users. As the ERM workflow belongs to the servicing librarians, a training programme should be conducted by an ERMS provider to help all servicing librarians understand the basics of e-resources, so that they can learn how to use them. With appropriate training, the resources can be put to a vast range of uses so that the money that has been spent developing and maintaining them can be justified. Training imparted to users can be propagated in numerous ways, including interactions through phone, e-mails, and other such electronic mediums. Formal library interaction sessions can also be organized throughout the year to make this happen.

It is also suggested that the ERM course should be introduced into the MLIS programme. Thus, the new librarians will have the opportunity to learn the specifics of their part in the ERM workflow while on the job. It is vital to understand the crucial aspects of the system so that improvement in the work of the colleagues can eventually lead to ERM efficiency. All the students preparing for librarianship would benefit from understanding the big picture of ERM.

REFERENCE

[1] T. Sadeh, M. Ellingsen, Electronic resource management systems: the need and the realization, New Library World 106 (5/6) (2005) 208–218.

CHAPTER 7

Implementation of Electronic Resource Management in Libraries: A Case Study

The need for academic libraries has been expanding with the growing competition among academic service providers. The competition among management institutions/business schools in India is based on how to attract students from all over the globe, and in the process compels them to strengthen the academic infrastructures of the organizations. Here, a factor that deserves mention is the presence of academic infrastructure within libraries. With this background, this study attempts to examine the differences prevailing in the status and strength of e-resources in India, along with the management practices existing in the top management institutes.

Analysis has been undertaken along with the testing of hypotheses using appropriate statistical tools related to the management of e-resources in the libraries of selected management institutes/business schools in India. This chapter highlights the need for study in the sphere of e-resource management. It also provides the perfect backdrop against which the study has been rationalized. The present study has been elaborated to focus upon the central idea of the study, which intends to appraise the e-resource management practiced in management institute/business school libraries in India. The motivation to carry out the study comes from the rational nature of the question framed for carrying out the study. These are followed by the objectives and hypotheses. The research rigor followed in the study is also discussed. Since research design is the backbone of research, its elaboration further strengthens the pursuit of research objectives.

7.1 MOTIVATION BEHIND THE STUDY

With the rapid changes in technology, there has been a shift in the methods of management which aim to deliver e-resources in libraries. Proper management of e-resources is indispensable, not only for optimal

Digital Disruption and Electronic Resource Management in Libraries.
DOI: http://dx.doi.org/10.1016/B978-0-08-102045-6.00007-8

usage, but also for providing the right information to the right user in the right manner.

How do libraries of management institutes manage their e-resources? Most of the research conducted earlier found that there is a gap between the management of print and e-resource collections of the libraries of management institutes in India. In addition to this, existing literature in this area reveals that no such comprehensive study has so far been conducted on e-resource management. Thus, the issues relating to managing the e-resources of sample libraries of management institutes in India have been identified. This study is an attempt to examine how e-resources are being managed in 38 sample libraries of management institutes in India.

7.2 THE PRESENT STUDY

During the last decade, providing access to e-resources has increased in libraries which has had a far-reaching impact on its users. The function of libraries has witnessed changes, including the impact of the fact that the e-resource can come from commercial publishers/vendors, open source, or a local digitization effort. The library allocates funds for commercially available e-resources, whereas open source e-resources are available freely on the web. Though the e-resources available in the library are increasing rapidly, the policies and procedures adopted for the purpose of their management has serious loopholes.

Thus, the present study intends essentially to evaluate the Electronic Resource Management (ERM) practices in libraries of management institutes in India. Based on the all-India ranking of management institutes, for the present study, libraries are classified into the following four groups (Table 7.1).

1. Top 10 ranked management institutes;
2. 11th to 20th ranked management institutes;
3. 21st to 30th ranked management institutes; and
4. 31st to 38th ranked management institutes.

Table 7.1 Groups of ranked management institutes in India

Sl. no.	Groups of ranked management institutes				Total
1	Top 10	11th to 20th	21st to 30th	31st to 38th	
2	10	10	10	8	38
Percentage	26.31	26.31	26.31	21.05	100.0

It is generally perceived that libraries of management institutes in India are more or less homogenous in adopting and implementing ERM practices. In order to validate this popular belief, the present study is carried out using different components of ERM.

7.3 RESEARCH QUESTIONS

To carry out the study, the following research statement have been developed:

1. The e-resource collection development process is an integral part of any modern library. It is considered to be well-recognized, and therefore in any academic library it helps to achieve better e-resource collections. It thus ensures better academic growth for its users, along with better institutional research output. In this context, it is important to investigate whether libraries in management institutes of India are maintaining any variation with regard to e-resource collection and development.

2. The library follows the standard structure for a better and sustainable process of lifecycle of e-resource management. These structures and norms ensure optimal use of the library budget and usage of e-resources by the users. But the question is, how many management institute libraries in India have been following the standard norms of lifecycle, and to what extent does it vary across the institutes?

3. The IT infrastructure is the prerequisite parameter for the management of e-resources. The better the IT infrastructure, the better will be the e-resource management. What is the level and extent of variation in IT infrastructure used/adopted in the libraries of management institutes in India?

4. The system/tools designed for managing the entire lifecycle of e-resources is an Electronic Resource Management System (ERMS). Have ERMS been implemented in the libraries in the study? How are the libraries managing their e-resources?

Keeping in mind the above questions, an appropriate structured questionnaire has been designed based on the nature, scope, and objectives of the study. Since the questionnaire is designed keeping in mind the management aspect of e-resources, it is divided into five different sections: (1) General Information, (2) E-resource Collection Development, (3) Lifecycle of E-resources, (4) IT Infrastructure, and (5) ERMS. Each section represents the relevant facets of the study.

7.4 OBJECTIVES

The study is based on the management of e-resources of libraries of top ranked management institutes in India according to their classification as mentioned above. The present study attempts to ascertain the following objectives:

1. To evaluate the e-resource collection development practiced in the libraries of the management institutes under study.
2. To assess the lifecycle of e-resource (selection, evaluation and assessment, acquisition, access, and renewal/cancelation) practiced in the libraries of management institutes under study.
3. To evaluate the IT infrastructure implemented in the libraries of management institutes under study.
4. To assess the ERMS practiced in the libraries of management institutes, or any alternative system adopted.

7.5 HYPOTHESIS

In view of the objectives of the study, the following hypotheses have been formulated:

H1: E-resources collection "development in libraries of management institutes do not vary significantly."

H2: "Total collection of e-resources," "number of library professionals trained on ERM," and "dedicated librarians" have a significant bearing on better methods adopted for the lifecycle of e-resources.

H3: Better management of e-resources is significantly affected by a vector of IT infrastructure facilities in the library such as: (1) number of servers and workstations, (2) internet speed, (3) dynamic website, (4) types of website, and (5) proportion of nonprofessional to total staff.

H4: There is homogeneity across the libraries under study to access and manage e-resources via A-to-Z list, subject list, library portal, OPAC, and federated/discovery search engine.

H5: No single libraries of management institutes in India are using ERM system/software for the management of electronic resources.

7.6 SCOPE OF THE STUDY

The present study is confined to only 38 libraries belonging to ranked management institutes in India. The study is confined to issues relating to e-resources collection development, status of IT infrastructure, lifecycle process of e-resources, and tools and technology implemented to manage e-resources.

This study is confined to only 38 ranked management institutions in India based on the reports published in three magazines (*Business India*, *Business World*, and *Business Today*) from the year 2009 to 2012. These three magazines conduct surveys each year to identify the ranked management institutes in India.

7.7 LIMITATIONS OF THE STUDY

The present study is an evaluative study. Utmost care has been taken to minimize errors; however, there will always be limitations. There may be limitations in the study as far as the theme and the coverage is concerned. A few important limitations of the present study are listed herewith.

As the present study is an evaluative study, it merely examines the nuances of e-resource management in libraries.

1. This study is conducted only in libraries of those institutes offering management education at postgraduate levels in the country.
2. This study is confined to only 38 ranked management institute libraries in India and therefore, other institutes of management education are not included in the sample.
3. The responses came from librarians of the sampled libraries of these institutes, therefore, this study includes their views only and not those of library users.

7.8 DESIGN OF THE STUDY AND METHODOLOGY

Perhaps there is no other aspect of management of products or services offered by the library in recent times that has received as much attention as the concept of e-resources. A wide gap has been observed in the understanding of the nuances of e-resource management in higher education institutions in general, and management education institutions in particular. Thus the present study, titled "Electronic Resource Management: A Case Study of Management School Libraries in India," is an attempt to address this gap.

This section intends to present the research method adopted in this study, and the plan for the entire research activity, including sampling, data collection, and the statistical methods applied to understand such material.

7.8.1 Research Design

A research design is a framework or blueprint for conducting a research project. It details the procedures necessary to obtain the information needed to structure and/or solve research problems. The research design lays the foundation for conducting the project [1].

7.8.2 Sampling Design

This study uses convenient sampling methods, as the management institutes in India are many and are scattered around India. Therefore, using B-school rankings from the years 2009 to 2012, management institutes in India were identified.

The study is conducted in 38 sample libraries of top 50 ranked management institutes in India, surveyed by three well regarded national magazines, i.e., (1) *Business India*, (2) *Business World*, and (3) *Business Today*. Generally, these three magazines conduct surveys and rank institutes each year. The idea is to identify the top management institutes in India in overall ranking.

For selection of the sample of the present study, data has been collected from the above-mentioned magazines for the period 2009 to 2012. The top 50 ranked management institutes/schools, as ranked by each magazine in each of these years, was taken to create the first stage of the sample. Now, there is a 12*112 matrix table where 12 columns signify the rank of management institutes of three magazines in four different years, and 112 rows are the ranked management institutes in India. Institutes which appear at least five times in any of the 12 columns have been selected as the second stage sample. An average of all these second stage samples has been taken and put in ascending order to select the top 50 management institutes. Libraries of these top 50 management institutes are selected as the sample for the study.

A suitably designed questionnaire has been sent to the libraries of the above 50 top management institutes in India. With serious effort and constant pursuit, 38 completed questionnaires (including the top 21 ranked management institutes) were received from librarians, library in-charge personnel, and other responsible staff.

7.8.3 Data Collection

In the present study, data were collected from both the primary and secondary sources. A structured questionnaire method was used in the collection of primary data. Fifty questionnaires were distributed/circulated to the librarians/library-in-charge personnel of the top 50 management school libraries in India. Out of that 50, after constant requests, reminders, and even personal visits to different places in India, the researcher was able to collect 38 completed questionnaires. Around 70% of the questionnaires were received by e-mail, the rest came through the post, and some were collected personally. Besides the primary source, the researcher consulted a secondary source, i.e., the websites of management institute libraries in India, for the collection of information.

7.8.4 Data Processing and Analysis

Data collected from the librarians/library in-charge personnel managing e-resources in their libraries were entered into SPSS software for analysis. Further, coding and decoding of data was done for analysis. Simple cross tabulation, simple statistical tools like mean and standard deviations, and advanced statistical tools like ANOVA, chi-square test, multiple regression analysis, and multinomial logistics analysis were applied for analysis.

7.9 SECTION I: GENERAL INFORMATION

A holistic picture of the sample 38 libraries of management institutes in India is presented in this section to give a general understanding of the sample frame, with the help of some relevant variables.

The year of establishment of the libraries varies from 64 years ago to relatively newly established libraries (in the year 2008). This gives ample opportunity to understand the dynamics of differences in management of e-resources adopted and practiced in old and new libraries, in order to provide better services to users. For better understanding, libraries are divided into five groups in terms of their years of establishment: (1) less than 10 years, (2) between 11 and 20 years old, (3) between 21 and 30 years old, (4) between 31 and 40 years old, and (5) above 40 years old. These libraries are again classified into four groups as per their overall ranking, according to three magazines. These four groups of ranked libraries of management institutes in India are (1) top 10, (2) 11th to 20th, (3) 21st to 30th, and (4) 31st to 38th.

Out of 38 libraries, around 8% (03) libraries are less than 10 years old. Around 21% (08) of the libraries are 11−20 years old. Another 15.85% (06) of the libraries are 21−30 years old. Between 28.9% (11) and 26.3% (10) of the libraries are 31−40 years and above 40 years, respectively (Table 7.2).

The disaggregation of libraries in four groups of ranking (as described above) and their establishment is depicted in Fig. 7.1. It is reported that out of three libraries which have been recently established (<10 years old), one is in the 31st to 38th group, and two are in the 21st to 30th ranked libraries. Out of 10 libraries which are more than 40 years old, five are in the top 10 and 11th to 20th ranked groups, respectively.

Staff and library users are two important components of any library. Both are complementary and supplementary to each other. There is an

Table 7.2 Year of establishment of sample libraries

	Top 10	11th to 20th	21st to 30th	31st to 38th	Total
Less than 10 years old	0	0	2	1	3
Between 11 and 20 years old	3	0	2	3	8
Between 21 and 30 years old	1	3	1	1	6
Between 31 and 40 years old	1	2	5	3	11
Above 40 years old	5	5	0	0	10
Total	10	10	10	8	38

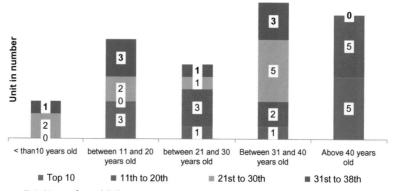

Figure 7.1 Year of establishment.

inverse relationship observed between the average number of staff and groups of ranked libraries. The better the rank of the libraries, the higher the average number of staff. It is also important to note that out of total staff, the proportion of professional staff to nonprofessional staff is higher in the case of better ranked groups. However, in the last ranked group of libraries, the proportion of professional staff is 66.7%, which is higher than the previous group of ranked libraries (Table 7.4).

The average number of library users in the top 10 ranked libraries is estimated to be 896, with 2346, 1078, and 1119 for the 11th to 20th, 21st to 30th, and 31st to 38th groups of ranked libraries, respectively. Estimation shows that the library users to total staff ratio increases with a decrease in the level of ranked library (Table 7.3).

There is a huge deviation observed in the case of number of library users, irrespective of the group of ranked libraries. The SD estimates for this variable are 352.4, 2829.6, 882.4, and 1544.6 for the top 10, 11th to 20th, 21st to 30th, and 31st to 38th group of ranked libraries, respectively. However, for other variables like professional, nonprofessional, and total staff, the deviation is more in the case of the top 10 and 11th to 20th ranked of group libraries and less in the case of the others (Table 7.4).

This implies that the last two groups of libraries are not only ranked less, but are also more or less homogeneous in their staffing patterns. At the same time, the top two groups of ranked libraries are not only better in terms of their ranking, but also they are very much heterogeneous.

To sum up, the above section basically is an attempt to justify the rationality of the sample. The samples are heterogeneous in terms of all four important indicators: (1) professional staff, (2) nonprofessional staff,

Table 7.3 Library staff and users

Groups of ranked libraries	Total staff SD (average)	% of professional staff to total staff	% of non-professional staff to total staff	Average number of library users	Library users to total staff ratio	Library users to professional staff ratio
Top 10	138 (13.8)	74.6	25.4	896	64.9	87.0
11th to 20th	135 (13.5)	57.8	42.2	2346	173.8	300.8
21st to 30th	80 (8)	60.0	40.0	1078	134.7	224.5
31st to 38th	48 (6)	66.7	33.3	1119	186.5	279.7

Note: SD, standard deviation, values in parentheses are average numbers.

Table 7.4 General information: average, minimum, maximum, and standard deviation

	Average	Minimum	Maximum	SD
Top 10 sample libraries of management institutes				
Number of library users	896	200	1500	352.4
Professional staff	10.3	4	25	6.4
Nonprofessional staff	3.5	0	17	5.2
Total staff	13.8	4	27	7.8
11th to 20th sample libraries of management institutes				
Number of library users	2346	100	9500	2829.6
Professional staff	7.8	3	25	6.4
Nonprofessional staff	5.7	2	12	3.06
Total staff	13.5	7	32	7.0
21st to 30th sample libraries of management institutes				
Number of library users	1078	150	3000	882.4
Professional staff	4.8	1	12	2.97
Nonprofessional staff	3.2	1	5	1.48
Total staff	8	2	17	4.08
31st to 38th sample libraries of management institutes				
Number of library users	1119	300	4900	1544.6
Professional staff	4	3	6	1.3
Nonprofessional staff	2	1	3	0.9
Total staff	6	4	7	1.1

SD, standard deviation.

(3) number of library users, and (4) year of establishment. With this background, with a heterogeneous sample frame, this study is an attempt to analyze the e-resources collection, development, and management in the libraries of management institutes in India. This may provide a pathway for a better management practice model for library professionals.

7.10 SECTION II: ELECTRONIC RESOURCE COLLECTION DEVELOPMENT

With the tremendous growth of information and the skyrocketing price of print resources, the library has resorted to e-resources collection development due to its easy accessibility and searchability, update speed, flexibility, and interactivity, etc. In addition, print resources take up a lot of space which libraries do not always have available. Furthermore, maintenance of the print resources is also a gigantic task for the library staff. Therefore, in order to avoid these problems, and for better management of resources, most libraries have been increasingly interested in espousing e-resource collection. Electronic resources consist mostly of e-books, e-journals, e-project reports, e-dissertations, e-theses, e-faculty presentations, e-faculty publications, open access e-resources, e-case studies, CD-ROMs, e-content pages, e-clippings, multimedia materials, geospatial e-resources, e-images, e-audio visuals, etc. [2].

Electronic resources "collection development" in libraries has been increasing significantly to meet the demand of users, to face competition, to attract students, and to provide facilities for better management.

This section is divided into two parts, in the first part a hypothesis is tested, and in the second part the growth of e-resources in the last 5 years, the number of online databases available in libraries, and the mode of access to e-resources is discussed.

7.10.1 Part One

7.10.1.1 Hypothesis 1

In order to test the hypothesis (*H1*), simple average, minimum, maximum, and SD tools are used. In addition, an ANOVA test has been conducted to reestablish the fact and measure the level of significance of the differences.

Differences have been observed: (1) across groups and (2) sampled as a whole through the above-mentioned tools for all indicators separately. As discussed, libraries are divided into four groups: (1) top 10 ranked, (2) 11th to 20th, (3) 21st to 30th, (4) 31st to 38th, and differences have been observed across these groups.

There were observed differences between various groups of ranked libraries in the top management institutes of India in terms of mean, minimum, maximum, and SD of different e-resources collection. However, no trend was observed in collection development of e-resources across these groups.

The average number of e-book collections was estimated to be 16,444 for all libraries, which varies from 39,685 for the group of top 10 libraries, to 1827 for the group of 31st to 38th ranked libraries. The SD increases with the increase in the rank of the group of libraries, indicating increasing variation among different groups of libraries. It is 1790 for the group of 31st to 38th ranked libraries, 8389 for the 21st to 30th group, 25,579 for the 11th to 20th group, and 55,841 for the top ranked libraries. A clear trend emerged on e-book collection development: (1) the average number of collection increases with an increase in the rank of the group of libraries and (2) variations in e-book collection development also increases with the increase in the rank of group of libraries captured through SD.

Electronic journal collection is high (8953) in libraries coming under the 11th to 20th ranked group, followed by the 31st to 38th ranked group (6831), top 10 (5060), and 21st to 30th ranked group (4567). There is wide variation observed in the case of this variable across and within the groups. A more or less similar trend has been observed in the case of e-project reports. As far as the e-dissertation is concerned, the average number of e-dissertations is 1275 for libraries from the 21st to 30th groups, followed by the 11th to 20th ranked group (1200), and the top 10 ranked group (296). Except for the 11th to 20th ranked group of libraries, there is no variation in e-dissertation collection development within other groups. However, there are variations that have been observed across groups in e-dissertation collections development.

In a similar way, variations in e-theses, e-faculty presentations, e-faculty publications, open e-resources, e-case studies, CD-ROMs, e-content pages, e-clippings, multimedia materials, geospatial resources, and CD-ROMs with databases, are observed in collection development both within and across different ranked libraries (Table 7.5).

7.10.1.2 Analysis of Variance

A one-way analysis of variance (ANOVA) is used to determine whether there are any significant differences between the means of three or more independent (unrelated) groups. In other words, it compares the varying means between the groups, and determines whether any of them bear any significant difference from each other.

7.10.1.3 How It Is Done

What ANOVA looks at is the way groups differ internally versus what the difference is between them. To take the above example:

1. ANOVA calculates the mean for each of the final groups: the group means.
2. It calculates the mean for all the groups combined: the overall mean.
3. Then it calculates, within each group, the total deviation of each individual's score from the group mean: within group variation.

Table 7.5 Electronic resources collection development

E-resources		Top 10	11th to 20th	21st to 30th	31st to 38th	Total
E-books	Mean	39,685	15,363	6525	1827	16,444
	Maximum	150,000	70,000	18,000	3685	150,000
	Minimum	2	21	20	6	2
	Std deviation	55,841	25,579	8389	1790	34,025
E-journals	Mean	5060	8953	4567	6831	6314
	Maximum	20,000	20,000	9000	16,000	20,000
	Minimum	20	12	46	200	12
	Std deviation	6773	6926	3156	5236	5813
E-project reports	Mean	649	3837	594	2678	1747
	Maximum	1768	5012	1273	4584	5012
	Minimum	59	1500	30	1450	30
	Std deviation	970	2024	520	1673	1813
E-dissertations	Mean	296	1200	1275	−	993
	Maximum	296	1500	1275	−	1500
	Minimum	296	899	1275	−	296
	Std deviation	−	425	−	−	526
E-theses	Mean	105	1637	152	13	556
	Maximum	296	4000	250	15	4000
	Minimum	9	20	54	11	9
	Std deviation	165	2092	139	3	1241
E-faculty presentations	Mean	−	156	122	485	309
	Maximum	−	156	185	1000	1000
	Minimum	−	156	59	100	59
	Std deviation	−	−	89	464	353
E-faculty publications	Mean	883	229	84	185	365
	Maximum	1848	400	93	250	1848
	Minimum	360	57	74	40	40
	Std deviation	837	243	13	99	512
Open access e-resources	Mean	5691	668	4273	3404	3439
	Maximum	17,000	2000	8536	10,000	17,000
	Minimum	33	2	9	13	2
	Std deviation	9794	1154	6029	5713	5795
E-case studies	Mean	700	4100	419	559	1330
	Maximum	1000	8000	784	900	8000
	Minimum	400	200	73	217	73
	Std deviation	424	5515	356	483	2523
CD-ROMs	Mean	3381	10290	1367	1007	4132
	Maximum	11,462	74,008	3755	3000	74,008
	Minimum	600	459	253	40	40
	Std deviation	3973	25,752	1136	1090	13,378
E-content pages	Mean	3675	−	468	12,750	5631
	Maximum	7000	−	735	25,000	25,000
	Minimum	350	−	200	500	200
	Std deviation	4702	−	378	17,324	9846

(*Continued*)

Table 7.5 (Continued)

E-resources		Top 10	11th to 20th	21st to 30th	31st to 38th	Total
E-clippings	Mean	3817	500	469	6000	2698
	Maximum	10,000	500	802	6000	10,000
	Minimum	250	500	135	6000	135
	Std deviation	5376	–	472	–	3818
Multimedia	Mean	269	2000	517	80	442
materials	Maximum	600	2000	1000	125	2000
	Minimum	50	2000	213	40	40
	Std deviation	259	–	423	43	593
Geospatial e-	Mean	1	–	18	1	7
resources	Maximum	1	–	18	1	18
	Minimum	1	–	18	1	1
	Std deviation	–	–	–	–	10
CD-ROM with	Mean	34	208	18	151	80
database	Maximum	100	230	65	300	300
	Minimum	2	185	1	1	1
	Std deviation	42	32	26	172	110

4. Next, it calculates the deviation of each group mean from the overall mean: between group variation.
5. Finally, ANOVA produces the "F" statistic, which is the ratio of between group variation to the within group variation.

If the "between group variation" is significantly greater than the "within group variation," then it is likely that there is a statistically significant difference between the groups.

The statistical package tells whether the "F" ratio is significant or not.

All versions of ANOVA follow these basic principles, but the sources of variation get more complex as the number of groups and the interaction effects increase. Statistical Package for Social Science (SPSS) is used to analyze the data.

7.10.1.4 Interpretation of Results

The results in Table 7.6 showthe "F" values and the level of significance of different variables separately. The probability value for the "e-project report" and "e-multimedia materials" variables are estimated to be significant at a 0.05% level. In other words, the test result for these two variables is found to be statistically significant at a significance level of less than 0.05. *Hence the null hypothesis is rejected in the case of these two variables.*

Table 7.6 Variation in electronic resources collection development: one way ANOVA

Variables	Between the group/within the group	
	F	"p" Sig
E-books	1.408	0.268
E-journals	1.179	0.333
E-project reports	5.166[a]	0.021
E-dissertations	1.801	0.466
E-theses	1.141	0.406
E-faculty presentations	0.636	0.589
E-faculty publications	1.769	0.240
Open source e-resources	0.312	0.816
E-case studies	1.063	0.443
CD-ROMs	0.796	0.507
E-content pages	0.755	0.542
E-clippings	0.507	0.704
E-multimedia materials	12.26[a]	0.004
Geospatial e-resources	–	–
CD-ROMs with databases	3.299	0.058

[a]Denotes significant at the 0.05 level.

This test provides sufficient evidence to conclude that there is a significant difference that exists across different groups of ranking sample libraries, in terms of acquisition of e-project reports and e-multimedia materials.

7.10.1.5 Posthoc Analysis

Posthoc means "after the fact." Posthoc tests are designed for situations in which the researcher has already obtained a significant omnibus *F-test*, with a factor that consists of three or more means. Additional exploration of the differences among means is needed to provide specific information on which means are significantly different from each other. The posthoc tests help to determine if particular pairs of values are significantly different from each other. In other words, posthoc tests are the best way to showcase the significant differences that exist among group means.

7.10.1.6 Least Significant Difference Test

The original solution to this problem, developed by Fisher, was to explore and observe all possible comparisons of means comprising of one factor that would use the equivalent of multiple *t-tests*. This procedure was named the least significant difference (LSD) test [3].

As discussed, a significant difference exists across different groups of ranked libraries in terms of acquisition of e-project reports and e-multimedia materials. Therefore, a LSD posthoc test is carried out to pinpoint the source of the particular significant differences among group means.

During the follow-up procedure, the one way ANOVA of the group factor was statistically significant. The output shows the follow-up results with multiple comparisons among all possible group pairings on mean acquisition of e-project reports and e-multimedia materials with the LSD posthoc test.

7.10.1.7 Electronic Project Reports

The LSD results show that mean differences between the "top 10" and "11th to 20th"; and "11th to 20th" and "21st to 30th" groups are statistically significant ($p = .013$ and $p = .006$), but none of the other pairings are statistically significant. Thus, the main sources of the statistical significance of the group factor are the differences between the "top 10 and 11th to 20th"; and "11th to 20th" and "21st to 30th" groups of libraries (Table 7.7).

7.10.1.8 Electronic Multimedia Materials

The LSD results for e-multimedia materials cannot be performed, because at least one group has fewer than two cases. In other words, due to limited data, posthoc analysis is not possible for this variable.

Table 7.7 Multiple comparisons: dependent variable electronic project report least significant difference

(I) RANK_1	(J) RANK_1	(I−J) Mean difference	Std error	Sig	95% Confidence interval	
					Lower bound	Upper bound
Top 10	11th to 20th	−3188.3[a]	1056.9	0.013	−5543.3	−833.3
	21st to 30th	54.8	945.4	0.955	−2051.6	2161.2
	31st and above	−2029.0	1056.9	0.084	−4384.0	326.0
11th to 20th	Top 10	3188.3[a]	1056.9	0.013	833.3	5543.3
	21st to 30th	3243.1[a]	945.4	0.006	1136.8	5349.5
	31st and above	1159.3	1056.9	0.298	−1195.7	3514.3
21st to 30th	Top 10	−54.8	945.4	0.955	−2161.2	2051.6
	11th to 20th	−3243.1[a]	945.4	0.006	−5349.5	−1136.8
	31st and above	−2083.8	945.4	0.052	−4190.2	22.6
31st and above	Top 10	2029.0	1056.9	0.084	−326.0	4384.0
	11th to 20th	−1159.3	1056.9	0.298	−3514.3	1195.7
	21st to 30th	2083.8	945.4	0.052	−22.6	4190.2

[a]The mean difference is significant at the 0.05 level. Multiple Comparisons.

7.10.2 Part Two

7.10.2.1 List of Online Databases Available in Libraries

It is reported that 205 types of online database are available to all libraries. These databases include e-books, e-journals, e-theses, e-project reports, etc. It is reported that most of the libraries have subscribed to Capitaline, CMIE database, Crisil research, EBSCO, Emerald, Indiastat.com, ISI emerging market, J-gate, JSTOR, PROQUEST, Science Direct, and Springer online resources.

7.10.2.2 Mode of Access to Electronic Resources

Above online databases/e-resources are accessed through three different modes: (1) IP-based, (2) user ID and login, and (3) both IP-based and user ID and login. Out of 38 libraries, all reported using IP-based modes to access e-resources. However, 89% of libraries reported using user ID login-based methods. These 34 libraries also reported using both methods simultaneously (Fig. 7.2 and Table 7.8).

7.10.2.3 Growth of Electronic Resources in Libraries

In this part, the growth of different types of e-resources is analyzed in order to understand the level of interest in e-resources by different groups of libraries. Three types of growth rates have been calculated to capture the pace of growth of different e-resource in libraries, including:

1. Year-to-year growth rate;
2. Average annual growth rate; and
3. Annual compound growth rate.

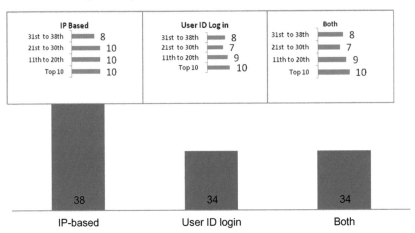

Figure 7.2 Mode of access to electronic resources.

Table 7.8 Mode of access to electronic resources

Group of ranked libraries	IP-based		User ID login		Both	
	Yes	No	Yes	No	Yes	No
Top 10	10	0	10	0	10	0
11th to 20th	10	0	9	1	9	1
21st to 30th	10	0	7	3	7	3
31st to 38th	8	0	8	0	8	0
Total	38	0	34	4	34	4

1. Year-to-year growth rate can be estimated using the formula below.

   To calculate the year-to-year growth rate of e-resources in the libraries of management institutions under study, two numbers are required. Then the following steps can be estimated.

   a. Subtract last year's number from this year's number. This gives the total difference for the year. Hopefully, it is positive and indicates year-to-year growth, not loss.

   b. Then, divide the difference by last year's number.

   c. This gives the year-to-year growth rate.

$$\{(P_t - P_{t-1})/P_{t-1} * 100\}.$$

2. The average of the above growth rate gives the annual average growth rate (average of year-to-year growth rate).

3. Annual compound growth rate can be estimated using the following methods:

   a. Natural logarithm of dependent variables.

   b. Regression of the converted values with the time/years (independent variable).

   c. Antilog (natural) of the "β" coefficient.

   Annual compound growth rate = $\{(\text{Antilog } \beta - 1) * 100\}$ [4]

7.10.2.4 Analysis of Growth of Electronic Resources

It is well accepted that base year value has an impact on the value of growth rate. Two types of growth rate have been estimated here on all e-resources for each group of libraries: (1) average annual growth rate, and (2) annual compound growth rate. There is no unique pattern observed as far as the rate of growth of the e-resources is concerned.

It has been estimated through detailed study that for the 11th, 20th, 21st, and 30th ranked groups, the rate of growth of e-books in libraries has reached three digit figures. It can, however, be said that the figures are so because of the base year value. The growth of the e-database has been observed to be the highest, i.e., 22.1% per annum in the 21st to 30th ranked library groups. They are then followed by the 31st to 38th (13.9%) ranked group. The growth percentage of e-databases in the top 10 ranked libraries has been found to be 7.3%. In fact, the second and fourth groups of libraries have reported an increasing accumulation of e-journals when compared to the other two ranked groups. The rate of growth of e-journals in the 2nd and 4th groups of libraries grows at an annual rate of 20.9% and 22.1%, respectively. The rate of growth of e-thesis collections is highest in the top 10 ranked libraries, followed by the 21st to 30th ranked. The figures for the 31st to 38th ranked groups of libraries are found to be highest at 61.6%, but the estimates are based on only 2 years of data. The CD-ROM collection figure has grown at the rate of 89.6% per annum in the 11th to 20th ranked libraries, followed by 35.0% in the top 10 ranked group of libraries, and at a rate of 16.2% per annum for the other two groups (Table 7.9). Therefore, the rate of growth of different e-resources across different group of ranked libraries varies.

7.11 SECTION III: LIFECYCLE OF ELECTRONIC RESOURCES

In this section, the lifecycle of e-resources is discussed in detail, including who uses the e-resources, different methods used for the selection and evaluation process of e-resources, followed by stages of acquisition and criteria/methods adopted for renewal/cancelation. There is as such no standard or norm that libraries need to follow for using specific methods/ criteria for different components of the e-resources lifecycle. However, Refs. [2,4−7] show that to ensure perfection in the process of selection, evaluation, acquisition, and renewal/cancelation, major criteria/methods need to be taken into consideration.

Access to e-resources for students and faculties are reported to be 100% in all groups of ranked libraries. However, there is no provision to ensure access to e-resources for all aspirants in different groups of libraries. The top 10, 11th to 20th, and 30th to 38th ranked groups of libraries have the provision to provide full access to e-resources to researchers. In the case of a few selective libraries, other groups access to e-resources have been reported to be less, as users in such categories were perhaps not available. In the same context, there is no provision for access to

Table 7.9 Growth of electronic resources in libraries

	Top 10	11th to 20th	21st to 30th	31st to 38th
E-books				
2009 over 2008	44.2	16.7	42.8	30.3
2010 over 2009	21.3	21382.9	44.7	10.7
2011 over 2010	10.1	73.9	2565.5	4.4
2012 over 2011	24.6	722.5	71.2	8.6
Average annual growth	25.0	5549.0	681.0	13.5
Annual compound growth rate	23.4	830.0	263.3	12.7
E-databases				
2009 over 2008	8.6	17.0	10.8	10.9
2010 over 2009	0.3	5.5	34.1	17.6
2011 over 2010	7.6	6.9	30.9	10.0
2012 over 2011	7.6	12.1	5.6	13.6
Average annual growth	6.0	10.4	20.4	13.0
Annual compound growth rate	7.3	9.4	22.1	13.9
E-journals				
2009 over 2008	8.8	7.2	17.0	7.4
2010 over 2009	0.6	40.5	− 7.9	19.3
2011 over 2010	22.2	18.4	11.6	47.0
2012 over 2011	0.1	14.0	12.1	3.9
Average annual growth	7.9	20.0	8.2	19.4
Annual compound growth rate	8.3	20.9	6.2	22.1
E-theses				
2009 over 2008	6.8	18.4	4.5	—
2010 over 2009	7.9	24.9	54.8	—
2011 over 2010	7.7	5.9	17.4	—
2012 over 2011	232.8	15.7	28.7	—
Average annual growth	63.8	16.2	26.4	—
Annual compound growth rate	35.0	16.2	27.1	61.6
CD-ROMs				
2009 over 2008	26.1	9.6	18.4	24.1
2010 over 2009	25.8	16.1	22.7	8.8
2011 over 2010	22.8	6.6	12.6	17.9
2012 over 2011	78.0	1498.6	18.7	13.6
Average annual growth	38.2	382.7	18.1	16.1
Annual compound growth rate	35.0	89.6	16.2	16.2

Table 7.10 Who accesses electronic resources

Type of users		Top 10	11th to 20th	21st to 30th	31st to 38th
Students	No	0	0	0	0
	Yes	10	10	10	8
Faculty	No	0	0	0	0
	Yes	10	10	10	8
Staff	No	1	5	2	3
	Yes	9	5	8	5
Researchers	No	0	0	3	0
	Yes	10	10	7	8
Library visitors	No	3	5	6	5
	Yes	7	5	4	3
Visiting faculties	No	2	2	4	2
	Yes	8	8	6	6
Distance education	No	7	9	8	7
faculties	Yes	3	1	2	1
Alumni	No	5	6	5	5
	Yes	5	4	5	3

e-resources in a few libraries of different ranked groups of libraries for library visitors, visiting faculties, distance education faculties, and alumni (Table 7.10).

7.11.1 Methods Used for Selection of Electronic Resources

To ensure consistency in approach with regard to print resources, selection of e-resources for inclusion into collections is an important role for a librarian. The methods used for selection of e-resources in the libraries of management institutes are depicted in Table 7.11. It has been reported that 100% of libraries in all groups follow "faculty suggestions" while selecting the e-resources for their collection. Trial offers and demonstrations from publisher vendors are also utilized by a majority of libraries, irrespective of their rank. Whereas only 10% of the top 10 group of libraries follow "discussion list" and "peer library website," and the 21st to 30th ranked group of libraries followed "publisher's catalogue," "from other libraries of similar nature," and "colleagues' suggestions."

Moreover, it has been noted that all nine methods were adopted by only one library in the top 10 group. There are only three libraries that follow two methods for selection of e-resources. It is also reported that 11 libraries follow three methods, seven libraries use four methods, six libraries follow five methods, three libraries use six methods, three

Table 7.11 Method used for selection of electronic resources

Methods used for selection of e-resources	Top 10 (%)	11th to 20th (%)	21st to 30th (%)	31st to 38th (%)
Trial offer	80	80	100	75
Demonstrations from publisher/vendors	80	100	90	100
Faculty suggestions	100	100	100	100
User recommendation	80	80	40	50
Discussion lists	10	30	0	12.5
Peer library website	10	30	20	25
Publisher's catalogue	50	20	10	25
From other library of similar nature	30	40	10	37.5
Colleagues' suggestions	30	30	10	12.5

Table 7.12 Number of methods used for selection of electronic resources

Group of ranked libraries	One	Two	Three	Four	Five	Six	Seven	Eight	Nine	Total
Top 10	1	1		3	2	1	1		1	10
11th to 20th		2		2	2	2		1	1	10
21st to 30th			7	1	1			1		10
31st to 38th			4	1	1		2			8

libraries use seven methods, two libraries use eight methods, and all nine methods are used by only two libraries for selection of e-resources (Table 7.12).

7.11.2 Evaluation Process for Selection of Electronic Resources

There are many e-resources available in the market which are contending, apparently comparably, and these resources are changing and evolving on a regular basis. It is difficult for the organization to decide which product is more needed than a competing one, or which product is better than the rest. Hence, the methods used for evaluation of the selection of e-resources is a challenging task for the librarian. There are 12 methods taken into account for the evaluation process for the selection of e-resources.

Table 7.13 Methods used for the evaluation process for the selection of electronic resources

Methods used for the evaluation process for selection of e-resources	Top 10	11th to 20th	21st to 30th	31st to 38th
Type of e-resources, such as full-text, bibliographic, abstract, etc.	9	10	10	8
Based on curriculum and research work	10	10	10	8
Reputation of the publisher	9	8	8	5
Intellectual level and quality of information	9	10	8	7
Indexing upgrades	9	6	7	5
Impact factor	9	10	5	4
Easy to access	9	9	10	7
Effectiveness (availability, back files, future upgrades, etc.)	10	10	10	6
Cost factor	8	10	7	6
Technical support	7	9	9	7
Consortia-based e-resources	8	9	8	7
Licensing agreement	8	10	9	5

Out of the 12 types of evaluation process discussed here, all libraries select e-resources based on curriculum and research work. Effectiveness is a method mostly followed by libraries for selection. During selection, types of e-resources as a basis are followed by almost all libraries except one library in the top 10 ranked group. The detail of the criteria followed by libraries is depicted in Table 7.13.

It is reported that all libraries follow at least a minimum of four evaluation processes for selection of an e-resource. Around 15 libraries have reported adopting all 12 methods for selection. In the top 10 ranked group, 90% of the libraries (9) follow at least 9 methods. A similar trend has been observed in the case of the 11th to 20th ranked groups of libraries. However, around 50% and 37.5% libraries in the 21st to 30th, and 31st to 38th ranked groups of libraries take into consideration more than 11 methods for the evaluation process for selection of e-resources (Table 7.14).

7.11.3 Process of Acquisition of Electronic Resources

Generally it is considered that a majority of libraries undertake the following four steps during the acquisition of e-resources: (1) verify the

Table 7.14 Number of methods used for the evaluation process for selection of electronic resources

Number of methods	Top 10	11th to 20th	21st to 30th	31st to 38th	Total
Four	0.0	0.0	0.0	12.5(1)	2.6(1)
Six	0.0	0.0	0.0	12.5(1)	2.6(1)
Seven	0.0	0.0	20.0(2)	0.0	5.3(2)
Eight	10.0(1)	10.0(1)	0.0	0.0	5.3(2)
Nine	30.0(3)	0.0	20.0(2)	12.5(1)	15.8(6)
Ten	0.0	0.0	10.0(1)	25.0(2)	7.9(3)
Eleven	20.0(2)	50.0(5)	10.0(1)	0.0	21.1(8)
Twelve	40.0(4)	40.0(4)	40.0(4)	37.5(3)	39.5(15)
Total	100.00(10)	100.00(10)	100.00(10)	100.00(8)	100.00(38)

Table 7.15 Methods used to verify the bibliographic information while acquiring electronic resources

Group of ranked libraries	For acquisition, % of libraries which verify the bibliographic information of e-resources	Out of which, % of institutions used the criteria			
		Contain provider of the product	Coverage	Frequency of update	Cost
	(1)	(2)	(3)	(4)	(5)
Top 10	100	80	90	90	90
11th to 20th	100	60	100	70	50
21st to 30th	100	70	90	80	70
31st to 38th	87.5	75	75	62.5	50

Note: Addition of figures in columns 2–5 will not be 100% because most of the institutions follow more than one method.

bibliographic information of the product, (2) identify the various pricing options, (3) review the license agreement, and (4) order and acquire the product.

Except for the 31st and the 38th ranked group libraries, all the other libraries verify the bibliographic information of the e-resources available. Similarly, the figure is 100%, 70%, and 50% for the 11th to 20th ranked group, 90%, 80%, and 70% in the case of the 21st to 30th ranked groups, and 75%, 62.5%, and 50% in the case of the 31st to 38th ranked groups of libraries (Table 7.15).

Table 7.16 Number of methods used for verify the bibliography information while acquiring electronic resources

Group of ranked libraries	Criteria used			
	One	Two	Three	Four
Top 10	1	0	2	7
11th to 20th	1	2	5	2
21st to 30th	1	0	6	3
31st to 38th	3	0	1	4

It is reported that more numbers of methods/criteria have been used to verify the bibliographic information while acquiring e-resources with the increase in the rank of the libraries. In other words, the higher the rank of the library, the more numbers of methods that are used to verify the bibliographic information while acquiring e-resources. A trend is observed that the top 10 and 31st to 38th ranked groups of libraries are using more methods/criteria during verification of the bibliographic information of e-resources (Table 7.16).

It is reported that all libraries in differently ranked groups identify various pricing options during the acquisition of e-resources. All libraries use content access as the criteria for identifying various pricing options while acquiring an e-resource. The percentage of libraries using "product types" as a method for acquisition varies from 62.5% to 90% across different ranked libraries. In the same way, the percentage varies from 60% to 100% for yearly subscription or one time purchase. Institutional size as a criteria is used by very few libraries, irrespective of group ranking. Similarly, "number of users," "consortia deal," and "journal package deal" as criteria are used by more than 50% of libraries, irrespective of rank (Table 7.17).

Six libraries from various ranked groups have been using seven criteria for various options while acquiring e-resources. Six criteria are being used by four libraries. Maximum numbers of libraries (seven) have been using three or four criteria for various options while acquiring e-resources. Except for the 11th to 20th and 31st to 38th ranked groups of libraries, a positive relationship has been observed between the various ranks of the libraries and the varying criteria used. In fact, a loose trend has also been observed, which showed that libraries that belonged to better ranked groups were using more numbers of criteria while identifying various different pricing options for e-resources (Table 7.18).

Table 7.17 Methods used for identifying various pricing options while acquiring electronic resources

Group of ranked libraries	For acquisition, % of libraries identify various pricing option of e-resources	Product type	Yearly subscription or one-time purchase	Institutional size	Number of users	Consortia deal	Journal package deal	Content access
Top 10	100	80	100	20	70	80	50	100
11th to 20th	100	90	60	50	60	50	50	100
21st to 30th	100	80	70	20	50	90	60	100
31st to 38th	100	62.5	87.5	12.5	37.5	37.5	25	100

Table 7.18 Number of methods used for identifying various pricing options while acquiring electronic resources

Group of ranked libraries	Criteria used							Total
	One	Two	Three	Four	Five	Six	Seven	
Top 10	1	1	0	2	3	1	2	10
11th to 20th		1	4	1	1	2	1	10
21st to 30th	1	1	2	1	2	1	2	10
31st to 38th	1	2	1	3			1	8

Libraries very often review the license agreement while acquiring e-resources. It is reported that all libraries in different groups of ranking review the license and business agreement of e-resources at the time of acquisition. There are 12 methods used for reviewing the license agreement. It is reported that no method was used by all the libraries for reviewing the license agreement. However, there are methods, such as name of license materials, location, authorized users, copyright and fare use, perpetual access, and usage statistics, which are used by more than 60–70% of libraries. Likewise, confidentiality and indemnification are methods used by very few libraries for review of agreements while acquiring e-resources, irrespective of group ranking (Table 7.19).

It is reported that only two libraries have used all twelve methods for reviewing license agreements while acquiring e-resources. A majority of libraries have used five to ten methods for reviewing license agreements while acquiring e-resources (Table 7.20). No trends have been observed between the groups of ranked libraries and individual libraries for reviewing the license and business agreement of e-resources.

There are generally eight methods/criteria that libraries should follow for ordering and acquiring e-resources during acquisition. Except for one library (in the 21st to 30th ranked group), others have reported on

Table 7.19 Methods used for reviewing license agreement while acquiring electronic resources

Methods used for reviewing licensing agreement	Top 10	11th to 20th	21st to 30th	31st to 38th
For acquisition, % of libraries reviewing the license and business agreement of e-resources	100	100	100	100
Name of license materials	80	100	90	75
Locations	70	80	70	62.5
Authorized users	80	70	70	62.5
Copyright and fair use	70	70	60	75
Confidentiality	0	20	10	50
Cost of subscriptions	60	60	70	75
Governing law	60	50	40	37.5
Perpetual access	80	90	80	50
Liabilities of library	40	60	40	25
Terms of payment and termination	50	50	60	12.5
Indemnification	10	40	20	12.5
Usage statistics	80	70	80	75

Table 7.20 Number of methods used for reviewing license agreement while acquiring electronic resources

Group of ranked libraries	One	Two	Three	Four	Five	Six	Seven	Eight	Nine	Ten	Eleven	Twelve	Total
Top 10	2					1	2	2		3			10
11th to 20th		1			3		1		1	2	1	1	10
21st to 30th	1		1		1	1	1	2	1		2		10
31st to 38th	1			2	1	1		1	1			1	8

ordering and acquiring the e-resource product during acquisition. More than 80% libraries use the "Communicate to content provider and give IP address, and request user ID and password" for ordering and acquiring the e-resource product. Except for methods like "Notify the concern sanction for adding the e-resource in OPAC, website, and other tools," which is followed by less than 80% of libraries for ordering and acquiring the e-resource product, for all other methods more than 80% of libraries used ordering and acquiring the product of e-resources during acquisition (Table 7.21).

It is quite interesting to note that a majority of libraries used more than seven methods for ordering and acquiring the product of e-resources during acquisition (Table 7.22). A trend is observed that the higher the rank of groups of libraries, the higher the number of criteria used for ordering and acquiring the product of e-resources.

7.11.4 Methods Adopted for Renewal/Cancelation

Various factors affect the renewal/cancelation of e-resources, however, prominently, (1) ranking of database by acquiring usage statistics, (2) Cost−benefit analysis, (3) relevance to research work and curriculum, (4) uniqueness to avoid duplication, (5) committee recommendation, and (6) budget factors play an important role.

It is reported that 73.7% libraries consider ranking of database, 52.6% consider cost benefit, 76.8% relevance, 65.8% uniqueness, 73.7% recommendation, and 68.4% budget for renewal/cancelation of e-resources. It is also reported that most of the libraries have been considering more than one factor for renewal/cancelation of the e-resources (Fig. 7.3 and Tables 7.23 and 7.24).

Table 7.21 Methods used for ordering and acquiring while acquiring electronic resources

Group of ranked libraries	For acquisition, % of libraries ordering and acquiring the product of e-resources	Communicate to content provider and give IP address, and request user ID and password	Get stable URL of the product for access	Verify access of the purchase product and inform different departments	Notify the concern sanction for adding the e-resource in OPAC, website, and other tools	Schedule training on e-resources	After access id confirmed, provider sends invoice for payment	Review invoice as per agreement	Process payment
Top 10	100	80	80	100	70	90	70	80	80
11th to 20th	100	100	90	90	80	90	100	90	100
21st to 30th	90	90	60	80	50	70	60	70	80
31st to 38th	100	87.5	62.5	87.5	37.5	87.5	50	75	62.5

Table 7.22 Number of methods used for ordering and acquiring while acquiring electronic resources

Group of ranked libraries	Criteria used								
	One	Two	Three	Four	Five	Six	Seven	Eight	Total
Top 10	1			1			4	4	10
11th to 20th	1					1	4	5	10
21st to 30th			1		3	1	1	3	10
31st to 38th		1	1		2	1	1	2	8

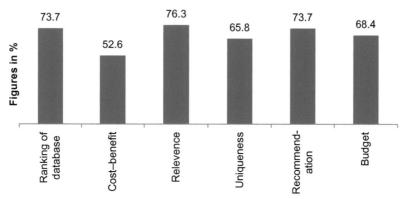

Figure 7.3 Methods adopted for renewal/cancelation of electronic resources.

Table 7.23 Methods adopted for renewal/cancelation of electronic resources

Group of ranked libraries	Ranking of database	Cost-benefit	Relevance	Uniqueness	Recommendation	Budget
Top 10	70.0	40.0	70.0	80.0	90.0	70.0
11th to 20th	90.0	40.0	70.0	60.0	70.0	80.0
21st to 30th	60.0	60.0	90.0	60.0	70.0	70.0
31st to 38th	75.0	75.0	75.0	62.5	62.5	50.0

Table 7.24 Definition, measurements, descriptive statistics and expected sign of variables used in the OLS (ordinary least square) equation

Variables	Description	Mean and (SD)	Expected sign
E_RE_C	Total number of collection of e-resources	26,597.89 (37,098.99)	+VE
Numbers training on ERM	Numbers of library staff undertaking training	1.0526 (1.137)	+VE
LIB_INC	0 = If a library is not headed by a full-time librarian, 1 = Otherwise	0.7368 (0.4463)	−VE

SD, standard deviation.

7.11.5 To Test Hypothesis 2

With the coefficient of e-resource collection being positive and highly significant, it appears that, on average, for every unit increase in e-resource collection, a 7.45 unit increase in the adoption lifecycle criteria is predicted. Similarly, for every unit increase in the numbers of library professionals undertaking training, a 4.05 unit increase in the adoption lifecycle criteria is predicted. However, the higher the adoption of lifecycle criteria is by a library if one moves from a library which is not headed by a full-time librarian to a library which is headed by a full-time librarian. In other words, a library with a full-time librarian has a better probability of adoption of life-cycle criteria than a library where the librarian is not a full-timer (Table 7.25). *Hence, the null hypothesis is accepted.*

7.12 SECTION IV: IT INFRASTRUCTURE

Infrastructure is a fundamental requirement for the establishment, growth, and development of any organization. It facilitates the organization to function at its optimum level. The IT infrastructure plays a crucial role in the management of libraries e-resources. Different IT infrastructures include: (1) hardware, (2) software, and (3) communication technology, such as computer, server, library software, website, and internet access which are all necessary for the management of e-resources in libraries.

7.12.1 Computer and Server Availability in Libraries

In order to understand the strengths and variation in hardware across different ranked groups of libraries, this study has selected the following eight variables: (1) central server, (2) workstations for users, (3) library automation server, (4) web server, (5) database server, (6) mail server, (7) CD-net server, and (8) institutional repository.

It is estimated that 84.2% of libraries have central servers, 97.4% have workstations for users, 94.7% have a library automation server,

Table 7.25 Determinants of number of criteria used by libraries for lifecycle of electronic resources

Variables	Coefficients	t-value
Constant	41.288	14.428
E_RE_C	7.450*	2.179
Numbers training on ERM	4.055*	3.676
LIB_INC	− 5.838*	− 2.063

Table 7.26 Numbers of computers and servers available in libraries

Computer and server	All (%)	Total	Min	Max	SD	N
Central server	84.2	43	1	3	0.65	32
Workstations for users	97.4	747	1	84	20.12	37
Library automation server	94.7	39	1	3	0.37	36
Web server	63.2	30	1	4	0.74	24
Database server	68.4	28.0	1.0	2.0	0.3	26
Mail server	57.9	24.0	1.0	3.0	0.4	22
CD–net server	31.6	12.0	1.0	1.0	0.0	12
Institutional repository	44.7	17.0	1.0	1.0	0.0	17
Any other	5.3	2.0	1.0	1.0	0.0	2

SD, standard deviation; Min, minimum; Max, maximum.

63.2% have a web server, 68.4% have a database server, 57.9% have a mail server, 31.6% have a CD–net server, 44.7% have an institutional repository, and 5.3% of libraries have other types of IT infrastructure in them. Apart from the above issues, the installation of different infrastructures in libraries depends upon their requirements. It is reported that IT infrastructures vary from 2 to 747 in numbers in aggregate across libraries. The minimum and maximum number of individual infrastructures varies from 1 to 84 across libraries. There is a high standard deviation (20.12) observed in the case of workstations for users (Table 7.26).

Disaggregated analysis across different libraries shows that not much difference has been observed in terms of use of IT infrastructure across different ranked libraries. Software used for managing e-resources is discussed in Section V of this chapter. All groups of libraries have a central server. The number varies between 7 (31st to 38th group) and 14 (11th to 20th group). There is a positive relationship observed between the number of workstations and the rank of the library. The higher the rank of the group, the higher the number of workstations, and vice versa. A similar trend is observed between other IT infrastructures and the rank of the library (Table 7.27).

7.12.2 Network Environment in Libraries

Communication technology is another important part of IT infrastructure. The significant aspects that comprise this technology include networking, internet access, and website development. One can easily

Table 7.27 Numbers of computers and servers available in ranked group of libraries

	All (%)	Total	Min	Max	SD	N
Top 10						
Central server	90.0	11	1.0	3.0	0.7	9
Workstations for users	100.0	266	2.0	84.0	26.7	10
Library automation server	100.0	12	1.0	3.0	0.6	10
Web server	80.0	12	1.0	4.0	1.1	8
Database server	70.0	8	1.0	2.0	0.38	7
Mail server	50.0	5	1.0	1.0	0.0	5
CD-net server	30.0	3	1.0	1.0	0.0	3
Institutional repository	30.0	3	1.0	1.0	0.0	3
Any other	0.0	0	0.0	0.0	0.0	0
11th to 20th						
Central server	90.0	14	1.0	3.0	0.9	9
Workstations for users	90.0	193	5.0	70.0	21.5	9
Library automation server	100.0	11	1.0	2.0	0.3	10
Web server	60.0	6	1.0	1.0	0.0	6
Database server	80.0	8	1.0	1.0	0.0	8
Mail server	60.0	6	1.0	1.0	0.0	6
CD-net server	50.0	5	1.0	1.0	0.0	5
Institutional repository	40.0	4	1.0	1.0	0.0	4
Any other	10.0	1	1.0	1.0	0.0	1
21st to 30th						
Central server	80.0	11	1.0	2.0	0.5	8
Workstations for users	100.0	155	1.0	50.0	14.7	10
Library automation server	80.0	8	1.0	1.0	0.0	8
Web server	40.0	6	1.0	3.0	1.0	4
Database server	60.0	6	1.0	1.0	0.0	6
Mail server	60.0	8	1.0	3.0	0.8	6
CD-net server	20.0	2	1.0	1.0	0.0	2
Institutional repository	50.0	5	1.0	1.0	0.0	5
Any other	10.0	1	1.0	1.0	0.0	1
31st to 38th						
Central server	75.0	7	1.0	2.0	0.4	6
Workstations for users	100.0	133	3.0	50.0	16.0	8
Library automation server	100.0	8	1.0	1.0	0.0	8
Web server	75.0	6	1.0	1.0	0.0	6
Database server	62.5	6	1.0	2.0	0.5	5
Mail server	62.5	5	1.0	1.0	0.0	5
CD-net server	25.0	2	1.0	1.0	0.0	2
Institutional repository	62.5	5	1.0	1.0	0.0	5
Any other	100.0	0	0.0	0.0	0.0	0

SD, standard deviation; *Min*, minimum; *Max*, maximum.

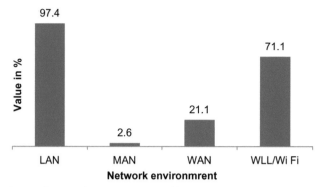

Figure 7.4 Type of network environment in libraries.

Table 7.28 Type of network environment in libraries

Group of ranked libraries	LAN	MAN	WAN	WLL/Wi Fi
Top 10	100.0	0.0	40.0	60.0
11th to 20th	100.0	10.0	20.0	80.0
21st to 30th	90.0	0.0	10.0	90.0
31st to 38th	100.0	0.0	12.5	50.0

exchange, transfer, and provide information through a network. The network environment plays a crucial role in the management of e-resources in libraries. It helps better management of e-resources and hence, qualitative services. A network with internet connection, type of internet connection, and speed of network (bandwidth) has been used in order to optimize user access to the libraries' resources.

It is reported that 97.4% of libraries have an LAN connection. Around 71.1% of libraries reported of having WLL/Wi Fi connectivity in their library; 21.1% and 2.6% of libraries reported having WAN and MAN connections (Fig. 7.4). The disaggregated analysis of different types of internet connection by different ranked groups of libraries is given in detail in Table 7.28.

7.12.3 Hypothesis 3

Variable specification

Both dependent and independent variables are discussed below.

7.12.4 Dependent Variable

It may be considered that better management of e-resources is important for: (1) easy accessibility, (2) containing duplication, (3) cost minimization, and (4) better time management. It will have a significant impact on a user's satisfaction, which may lead to optimal use of library resources and better research output. Better e-resource management has been defined in books after taking into consideration a few parameters. However, for this study: (1) access to e-resources through discovery/ federated search; (2) organization of e-resources via A-to-Z list, subject wise or containing types in the website; (3) access through OPAC, website, and federated search; (4) e-resource management by library automation software; (5) e-resource management by digital library software; and (6) CD-networking software to manage e-resources are considered.

As discussed, the dependent variable is a combination of a set of qualitative variables. Out of the six qualitative variables which constitute the major dependent variables, three (numbers 1−3) are single variables, where as of the rest, each variable (numbers 4−6) is a combination of separate sets of variables.

7.12.5 Estimation of Variables which Are Combinations of Sets of Variables

1. Library resources managed by automation software are a combination of seven qualitative variables: (1) books, (2) journals, (3) CD-ROM, (4) project reports, (5) theses, (6) dissertations, and (7) faculty publications.

   "Library resources managed by automation software" = 1, if the library is using automation software for the management of any one of the above variables, 0 = otherwise.
2. E-resources managed by digital library software are a combination of six qualitative variables: (1) faculty publications, (2) project reports, (3) theses, (4) dissertations, (5) lecture notes, and (6) question papers.

   "E-resources managed by digital library software" = 1, if the library is using digital software for the management of any one of the above variables, 0 = otherwise.
3. CD-networking software managed e-resources are a combination of four qualitative variables: (1) CDs/DVDs come with book, (2) educational CD/DVDs, (3) faculty presentations, and (4) company databases.

"CD-networking software managed e-resources" = 1, if the library is using CD-networking software for management of any one of the above variables, 0 = otherwise.

7.12.6 Estimation of Dependent Variable

"Better management of e-resources" = 1, if the library is using any five or more parameters for management of e-resources, 0 = otherwise.

7.12.7 Independent Variables

Management of e-resources has two components: (1) optimal management of resources by the library, and (2) offering the best access to users. To meet the desirability of both the components, the following variables are necessary.

1. *Numbers of servers and workstations*: In the days of information technology, most libraries have adopted the IT-based method for management. For efficient management of the library, servers and workstations are a prerequisite. Generally, one can see different types of models adopted by different libraries, such as, one server with many workstations, and many servers with many workstations. A higher number of servers and workstations has a positive implication for better management of e-resources.

2. *Internet speed*: After acquisition of e-resources, a challenge for the library to face is to provide uninterrupted access to the users "anywhere" and "anytime." Better internet speed (bandwidth) is the most suitable tool for accessing the e-resources, and can comply with the requirement for better management of the e-resources in the library. Generally, the probability of better management of e-resources is only possible with better internet speed.

3. *Types of website*: A library website is a gateway to information about library resources. A dedicated library website with multiple pages offers better provision for management.

4. *Dynamic website*: A dynamic website facilitates: (1) easy content updates, (2) searching, and (3) user participation, which are indispensable components of better management. There is a positive correlation between a dynamic website and better e-resources management.

5. *Proportion of nonprofessional to total staff*: Both professional and nonprofessional staff are equally important for the management and functioning of a library. Better e-resource management requires expertise in

Table 7.29 Basic characteristics of independent variables for hypothesis 3

		No. of servers and work stations	Internet speed (Kbps)	Dynamic website	Type of website	Proportion of nonprofessional to total staff
Sum	Better managed	582	8,587,271	12	7.0	5.6
	Other	358	3,400,701	2	9.0	7.9
Avg	Better managed	32	477,071	1	0.4	0.3
	Other	18	170,035	0	0.5	0.4
Min	Better managed	2	14	0	0.0	0.0
	Other	1	256	0	0.0	0.1
Max	Better managed	87	1,048,575	1	1.0	0.7
	Other	77	1,048,575	1	1.0	0.6
SD	Better managed	23	523646	0	0.5	0.2
	Other	16	379022	0	0.5	0.2

N:B; *Avg*, average; *Min*, minimum; *Max*, maximum; *SD*, standard deviation.

the area of IT. Hence, the acceptability and importance of professionals has increased due to their technical expertise in the area of IT. However, in the IT environment, an increasing proportion of nonprofessional to professional staff affects the e-resource management enormously.

Table 7.29 above indicates a close correspondence between IT infrastructure, library staff, and better management of e-resources. To confirm the magnitude of each independent variable on management of e-resources by a library, a multivariate logistic regression analysis is carried out. The general model is a binary choice model involving estimation of the probability of "a library is better managed or not" as a function of a vector of explanatory variables included in the "IT infrastructure and staffing pattern" vector. If P is the probability of a library being better managed then:

$$\text{Log}_e\left[P_i/1 - P_i\right] = \beta X = \sum \beta_j X_{ij} \quad (j=0-\,k)$$

Using the above expression, the log odds of a library being better managed as a linear function of the explanatory variables are calculated. Hence, it can be interpreted that the odd ratio [Exp (β)] in terms of the change in odds, i.e., if the value is greater than one, it indicates that as the predictor increases, the odds of the outcome occurring increases. Conversely, a value less than 1 indicates that as the predictor increases, the odds of the outcome occurring decreases. The estimated results are

Table 7.30 Result of logistic regression on better management of electronic resource

Variables	β coefficient	$E(\beta)$	SE
Number of servers and workstations	0.066**	1.06	0.035
Internet speed	3.106**	1.00	0.000001
Dynamic website	5.438*	230.10	2.012
Types of website	3.966**	52.78	1.921
Proportion of nonprofessional to total staff	− 4.676	0.009	3.832

− 2 log likelihood = 24.242, R^2 = 0.526 (Cox and Snell R Square), 0.701 (Nagelkerke R Square), number of observation = 38, χ^2 = 28.33.
Note: * and ** imply significance at 1% and 10% level respectively.

outlined in Table 7.30. Notably, all parameters reflect an expected association, and are statistically significant except one variable (proportion of nonprofessional to total staff).

7.12.8 Analysis of Results

The above analysis reveals that there is a positive relationship between a library having a number of servers and workstations, and their being better managed. As libraries with the numbers of 'servers and workstations' increases the probability of being better managed libraries increases. Similarly, libraries with higher internet speeds increase the probability of being better managed. There is a positive relationship observed between libraries with dynamic websites and libraries that are being better managed. For instance, ceteris paribus, the probability of such libraries being better managed is 230 times higher than those libraries without dynamic websites. As expected, in libraries with a dedicated library website with multiple pages, the probability of such libraries being better managed is 52.78 times more efficient compared to other libraries. Therefore, it can be concluded that e-resource management is significantly affected by a vector of IT infrastructure facilities in the library. *Hence the null hypothesis is accepted.*

7.13 SECTION V: ELECTRONIC RESOURCE MANAGEMENT SYSTEMS

In addition to the traditional print collection, management of e-resources has become quite a challenging task for professionals, because of the involvement of electronic materials, as well as collections of digital objects. To understand the management of e-resources by the libraries of management institutes in India, different factors have been taken into account, i.e., resources managed by the library automation software, digital library software, CD-networking software, A-to-Z list, subject wise, content type, access through OPAC, website, discovery/federated search engine, and ERMS.

7.13.1 Hypothesis 4
7.13.1.1 Chi-Square Test
A chi-square test is designed to analyze categorical data. That means that the data has been counted and divided into categories. It will not work with parametric or continuous data.

A chi-square test is a versatile statistical test used to examine the significance of relationships between two (or more) nominal-level variables. Here, a chi-square test is carried out to examine the association between four ranked groups of libraries and different types of e-resource management, such as: (1) A-to-Z listing, (2) subject wise, (3) content type, (4) access through OPAC, (5) access through the library web, and (6) access through federated search.

Table 7.31 Management of electronic resource via A-to-Z list, subject wise, content type, OPAC, library website, and federated search

Types of e-resource management		Top 10	11th to 20th	21st to 30th	31st to 38th	Total
A-to-Z listing	NO	1	5	2	5	13
	YES	9	5	8	3	25
Subject wise	NO	4	5	7	4	20
	YES	6	5	3	4	18
Content type	NO	5	8	9	5	27
	YES	5	2	1	3	11
Access through OPAC	NO	7	7	6	3	23
	YES	3	3	4	5	15
Access through library web	NO	1	1	1	4	7
	YES	9	9	9	4	31
Access through federated search	NO	6	7	10	7	30
	YES	4	3	0	1	8

Out of 38 libraries, 25 libraries manage e-resources by arranging A-to-Z listing. Similarly, 18 libraries manage using a "subject wise" method, 11 libraries use content type, and 15, 13, and 8 use access through OPAC, library website, and federated search engine, respectively (Table 7.31).

From the output of Tables 7.32 to 7.37 above, one can see here that χ (1) $= 7.454$ and $p = .059$, $\chi(2) = 4.574$ and $p = .206$, $\chi(3) = 1.900$ and $p = .593$, $\chi(4) = 2.528$ and $p = .470$, $\chi(5) = 6.724$ and $p = .081$, and $\chi(6) = 5.660$ and $p = .129$ variables, respectively.

Table 7.32 A-to-Z listing: chi-square tests

	Value	Df	Asymp. sig. (2-sided)
Pearson chi-square	7.454	3	0.059
Likelihood ratio	7.866	3	0.049
Linear-by-linear association	2.919	1	0.088
No. of valid cases	38		

Four cells (50.0%) have an expected count less than 5. The minimum expected count is 2.74.

Table 7.33 Subject wise: chi-square tests

	Value	Df	Asymp. sig. (2-sided)
Pearson chi-square	1.900	3	0.593
Likelihood ratio	1.943	3	0.584
Linear-by-linear association	.574	1	0.449
No. of valid cases	38		

Five cells (62.5%) have an expected count less than 5. The minimum expected count is 3.79.

Table 7.34 Content type: chi-square tests

	Value	Df	Asymp. sig. (2-sided)
Pearson chi-square	4.574	3	0.206
Likelihood ratio	4.770	3	0.189
Linear-by-linear association	.724	1	0.395
No. of valid cases	38		

Four cells (50.0%) have an expected count less than 5. The minimum expected count is 2.32.

Table 7.35 Access through OPAC: chi-square tests

	Value	Df	Asymp. sig. (2-sided)
Pearson chi-square	2.528	3	0.470
Likelihood ratio	2.502	3	0.475
Linear-by-linear association	1.976	1	0.160
No. of valid cases	38		

Five cells (62.5%) have an expected count less than 5. The minimum expected count is 3.16.

Table 7.36 Access through library website: chi-square tests

	Value	Df	Asymp. sig. (2-sided)
Pearson chi–square	6.724	3	0.081
Likelihood ratio	5.711	3	0.127
Linear-by-linear association	3.654	1	0.056
No. of valid cases	38		

Four cells (50.0%) have an expected count less than 5. The minimum expected count is 1.47.

Table 7.37 Access through federated search: chi-square tests

	Value	Df	Asymp. sig. (2-sided)
Pearson chi–square	5.660	3	0.129
Likelihood ratio	7.408	3	0.060
Linear-by-linear association	3.730	1	0.053
No. of valid cases	38		

Four cells (50.0%) have an expected count less than 5. The minimum expected count is 1.68.

If the "p" value is less than .05, then the statistic is considered to be significant. In other words, the researcher can be 95% confident that the relationship between the two variables is not due to chance. In this example, since all "p" values are greater than .05, there is no statistically significant association between rankings of libraries with different components of adoption of e-resources. *Therefore, the null hypothesis is accepted.*

7.13.1.2 Library Automation Software Used by Libraries

It has been reported that a majority of management institute libraries have been using LISYS library automation software. A few have also reported using in-house software for library automation. A list of other software used by different management institutes libraries for library automation is given in Table 7.38.

It has been reported that almost all libraries in management institutes have been using some software for the library automation process. With the help of this software, libraries are automating several different items in the library. It is reported that 100% "bibliography of books" is automated, followed by 86.8% of "bibliography of journals," 81.6% "bibliography of CD-ROMs," and so on. Very small amounts of full-text (2.6%), content page of CD-ROMs (5.3%), or content page of dissertations (5.3%), are reported to be automated by libraries of management

Table 7.38 Name of library automation software used by libraries

Name of the library automation software use	Name of management institutes libraries
Alice for windows	XLRI—Jamshedpur, NIM—Ahmedabad
Auto lib	LIBA—Chennai
E-Granthalaya	RCM—Bhubaneswar
In-house software	KJSIMSR—Mumbai, GLIM—Chennai, PSGIM—Coimbatore, TAPMI—Manipal
KOHA	IIM—Ahmadabad, SJMSM—IIT Mumbai, IFMR—Chennai
LIBSOFT	AIMS—Bangalore
Libsuite	SPJIMR—Mumbai, IBS—Hyderabad, WIMDR—Mumbai
LIBSYS	IIM—Kolkata, IIM—Luckow, IIM—Kozhikode, IIFT—Delhi, MDI—Gurgaon, NMIMS—Mumbai, IMT—Ghaziabad, NITIE—Mumbai, DMS—IIT Delhi, IMI—Delhi, IIFM—Bhopal, IRM—Anand, IMT—Nagpur
LIS	XIM—Bhubaneswar
NETTLIB/VIDYUT	LBSIM—Delhi
SLIM 21	SIMS—Pune
slim 21 + Any other please	SIMSREE—Mumbai
SOUL	JBIMS—Mumbai
Troodon 4.0	FMS—Delhi
VTLS	IIM—Bangalore, ISB—Hyderabad, IIM—Indore, IIM—Shillong

institutes. Except for a few items, there is a positive relationship observed between the rank of the libraries and the percentage of items automated (Table 7.39).

7.13.1.3 Digital Library Software Used by Libraries

It is reported that most of the libraries of management institutes are using DSpace digital library software. A few have also reported using GSLD, KOHA, Libsuite, and NETTLIB/VIDYUT for digitization of resources. However, a majority of libraries also reported not using any software for digitization (Table 7.40).

The libraries using software for digitization of resources include 70% (among the top 10), 40% (among the 11th to 20th ranked), 50% (among the 21st to 30th ranked), and 62.5% (among the 31st to 38th ranked).

Table 7.39 Percentages of items automated by library automation software

Items automated	Top 10 (%)	11th to 20th (%)	21st to 30th (%)	31st to 38th (%)	All
Bibliography of books	100	100	100	100	100
Content page of books	20	20	0	12.5	13.2
Full-text of books	10	0	0	0	2.6
Bibliography of journals	100	70	80	100	86.8
Content page of journals	40	10	20	12.5	21.1
Full-text of journals	20	10	10	0	10.5
Bibliography of CD-ROMs	100	80	50	100	81.6
Content page of CD-ROMs	20	0	0	0	5.3
Full-text of CD-ROMs	20	10	10	12.5	13.2
Bibliography of project reports	50	60	50	62.5	55.3
Full-text of project reports	10	10	0	12.5	7.9
Bibliography of theses	30	40	20	75	39.5
Content page of theses	10	10	10	0	7.9
Full-text of theses	10	20	10	25	15.8
Bibliography of dissertations	20	50	20	62.5	36.8
Content page of dissertations	10	10	0	0	5.3
Full-text of dissertations	10	30	0	12.5	13.2
Bibliography of faculty publications	60	60	10	50	44.7
Content page of faculty publications	20	10	0	0	7.9
Full-text of faculty publications	10	20	0	12.5	10.5
Total	100	100	100	100	100

Out of the libraries using software for digitization, in the top 10 group, 70% of the metadata of faculty publications are digitized, 40% of the full-text of faculty publications, full-text of project reports, and metadata of project reports is digitized. In the case of the other three groups, digitization of items are less than the top 10 ranked group of libraries (Table 7.41).

Table 7.40 Name of digital library software used by libraries

Name of digital library software used	Name of management institutes libraries
DSpace	IIM—Ahmadabad, IIM—Bangalore, XLRI—Jamshedpur, FMS—Delhi, IIM—Indore, IIFT—Delhi, MDI—Gurgaon, DMS—IIT Delhi, IMI—Delhi, GLIM—Chennai, RCM—Bhubaneswar, NIM—Ahmedabad, IMT—Nagpur, AIMS—Bangalore, IIM—Kozhikode
GSDL	IIM—Kozhikode, IIM—Luckow, IMT—Ghaziabad, TAPMI—Manipal
KOHA	SJMSM—IIT Mumbai
Libsuite	WIMDR—Mumbai
NETTLIB/VIDYUT	LBSIM—Delhi
No digital library software use	IIM—Kolkata, ISB—Hyderabad, SPJIMR—Mumbai, IBS—Hyderabad, JBIMS—Mumbai, NMIMS—Mumbai, NITIE—Mumbai, SIMS—Pune, XIM—Bhubaneswar, KJSIMSR—Mumbai, LIBA—Chennai, PSGIM—Coimbatore, IIM—Shillong, IIFM—Bhopal, IRM—Anand, IFMR—Chennai, SIMSREE—Mumbai

7.13.1.4 CD-Networking Software Used by Libraries

It is observed that a majority of management institutes are using "Lanbit FISC" and "Tulsient CD Storage Solutions" CD-networking software for their libraries (Table 7.42). It was also noticed that a major number of libraries are not using any CD-networking software.

On aggregate, 52.6% libraries have CD-networking software. The percentage is high for the 21st to 30th group (70%) and the top 10 group of libraries (60%). Out of libraries who have CD-networking software, 52.6% of CD/DVDs come with books, 47.4% of educational CD/DVDs, 28.9% of company databases, and 7.9% of faculty presentations are uploaded in CD-networking software. It is observed that the top 10 and 21st to 30th groups of libraries have taken a lead in uploading e-resources in CD-networking software (Table 7.43).

7.13.1.5 Discovery/Federated Search Engine Used by Libraries

Although a handful of libraries have reported the use of a Discovery/Federated search engine for conducting singular search for e-resources,

Table 7.41 Percentages of items digitized by digital library software

	Top 10	11th to 20th	21st to 30th	31st to 38th
Digital library software	**70**	**40**	**50**	**62.5**
Items digitized				
Content page of faculty publications	30	0	0	0
Full-text of faculty publications	40	20	20	37.5
Metadata of faculty publications	70	40	30	37.5
Content page of project reports	10	0	0	0
Full-text of project reports	40	20	30	50
Metadata of project reports	40	20	40	37.5
Content page of theses	0	10	10	12.5
Full-text of theses	30	10	30	50
Metadata of theses	30	30	30	50
Content page of dissertations	0	10	0	0
Full-text of dissertations	20	10	20	37.5
Metadata of dissertations	20	20	30	37.5
Content page of lecture notes	0	0	0	0
Full-text of lecture notes	0	0	10	12.5
Metadata of lecture notes	10	0	10	12.5
Content page of question papers	0	0	0	0
Full-text of question papers	0	0	10	0
Metadata of question papers	10	0	20	0

there is a majority that have not yet sought that option. (1) Chameleon iPortal, EBSCO Discovery Service, GIST FIND from Gist, and Summon (Table 7.44).

7.13.1.6 Hypothesis 5

A popular tool to manage the lifecycle of e-resources is ERMS. Several companies have developed ERM software which is available through commercial and open source systems. The implementation of ERM has

Table 7.42 Name of CD-networking software used by libraries

Name of CD-networking software use	Name of management institute libraries
VTLS, Virtua	IIM—Shillong
Beeges	FMS—Delhi
CDez network CD-ROM server	AIMS—Bangalore
Dbshare	IIM—Bangalore
Excel network attached storage	IMT—Ghaziabad
Lanbit FISC	IIM—Luckow, ISB—Hyderabad, IBS—Hyderabad, IIFT—DelhiDMS—IIT Delhi, SJMSM—IIT Mumbai, IMI—Delhi, RCM—Bhubaneswar, NIM—Ahmedabad, LBSIM—Delhi
Libsuite	WIMDR—Mumbai
Tulsient CD storage solutions	IIM—Indore, IIM—Kozhikode, NITIE—Mumbai, KJSIMSR—Mumbai
No software use	IIM—Ahemadabad, IIM—Kolkata, XLRI—Jamshedpur, SPJIMR—Mumbai, JBIMS—Mumbai, MDI—Gurgaon, NMIMS—Mumbai, SIMS—Pune, XIM—Bhubaneswar, GLIM—Chennai,LIBA—Chennai, PSGIM—Coimbatore, IIFM—Bhopal, IRM—Anand, IMT—Nagpur, IFMR—Chennai, TAPMI—Manipal, SIMSREE—Mumbai

Table 7.43 Electronic resource managed by CD-networking software

	Top 10	21st to 30th	21st to 30th	31st to 38th	All
CD-networking software	60	50	70	25	52.6
Items stored in CD-networking server					
CD/DVD comes with books	60	50	70	25	52.6
Educational CD/DVD	60	40	60	25	47.4
Faculty presentation	0	0	20	12.5	7.9
Company databases	30	20	50	12.5	28.9

Table 7.44 Name of discovery/federated search engine used by libraries

Name of discovery/federated search software use of e-resources	Name of management institute libraries
Chameleon iPortal	ISB—Hyderabad
EBSCO Discovery service	IIM—Ahemadabad, IIM—Kolkata, IIM—Indore, DMS—IIT Delhi, LBSIM—Delhi
EBSCO Discovery service (Trial access)	IIM—Luckow, IMT—Ghaziabad
GIST FIND from Gist	NITIE—Mumbai
GistFind	FMS—Delhi
Summon	IIM—Bangalore
No software use	XLRI—Jamshedpur, SPJIMR—Mumbai, IIM—Kozhikode, IBS—Hyderabad, JBIMS—Mumbai, IIFT—Delhi, MDI—GurgaonNMIMS—Mumbai, SIMS—Pune, XIM—Bhubaneswar, SJMSM—IIT Mumbai, KJSIMSR—Mumbai, IMI—Delhi, GLIM—Chennai, LIBA—Chennai, WIMDR—Mumbai, PSGIM—Coimbatore, IIM—Shillong, RCM—Bhubaneswar, IIFM—Bhopal, IRM—Anand, NIM—Ahmedabad, IMT—Nagpur,AIMS—Bangalore, IFMR—Chennai, TAPMI—Manipal, SIMSREE—Mumbai

several benefits, both for librarians and users. Keeping in mind this change, there are several internationally different institutions/organizations that have already started the implementation of ERMS.

To understand the implementation of ERMS in the Indian context, a study has been undertaken within this research. No libraries in management institutes in India have reported implementing ERMS. *Hence the null hypothesis is accepted.*

7.14 CONCLUSIONS

The concept of "library management" has been changing dramatically with the increase in the demand for academic input in education, policy planning, advocacy, and day-to-day life. Though it cannot be denied that shifting from "print resource collection" to "e-resource collection" makes the library considerably more user-friendly, it is a fact that these e-resources intensify the challenge for library personnel to adopt to rapidly changing ways. Electronic resources management is one of the important components of library development. After the automation and digitization of library resources is over, professional management of the vast body of e-resources is the next goal for its staff. The voluminous e-resource can easily be managed through an ERM system.

In this study, it has been observed that not all libraries are following all the steps of different components of ERM such as selection, evaluation, acquisition, license agreement, and renewal/cancelation of e-resources, which are essential for the better management of e-resources. The study also observed that there is a minimum level of hardware requirement for the efficient management of e-resources. However, there is a positive relationship observed between the groups of ranked libraries and their acquisition of computers and servers. In other words, the higher the group of ranked libraries, the higher the number of computers and servers. All libraries have internet connectivity. However, the speed of internet (bandwidth) varies from library to library, i.e., from 14 to 8,587,271 kbps. Even though all libraries have their own websites, the study states that most of them did not possess a dynamic website (63.2%). Similarly, a majority of libraries (57.9%) did not have a dedicated multiple-page website.

Even though it has been realized that the ERM system is an essential tool for management of e-resources, not a single sample library has adopted ERMS, even though they have implemented library automation and digitization software. On the other hand, the development of computer and communication infrastructure facilities is progressing. It is concluded that all libraries have been using their best efforts to increase computer infrastructure, because it helps in managing e-resources. Slow adoption of new technology may not be due to budget constraints, but is most likely due to the nonavailability of skilled personnel in the library.

It is well accepted that the computerization of the library is shifting from labor-intensive to capital-intensive methods. However, adoption of this method requires the development of personal skills. Most libraries in India are in such a phase where they are neither in a position to train the existing staff to handle technical operations, nor can they hire technically competent individuals. Therefore upgrading of skills is the only way to proceed. Hence, skilled training of their existing technical staff has become a priority for libraries.

A network facility is a prerequisite for the management of ERM in libraries. To realize this benefit, libraries in management institutes in India put in their best efforts to extend their networking facilities through more desktop devices, as well as higher internet speeds.

Hypothesis 1 concluded that a significant difference exists across different groups of ranking sample libraries in terms of acquisition of e-project reports and e-multimedia materials. In the case of hypothesis 2, it is concluded that with the coefficient of e-resource collection being positive and highly significant, with every unit increase in e-resource collection a significant increase in the adoption lifecycle criteria can be predicted. Similarly, for every unit increase in the number of library professionals undertaking training, the adoption lifecycle criterion is predicted to improve. Similarly, a library with a full-time librarian has a better possibility of adoption of lifecycle criteria than a library where the librarian is not a full-timer.

Hypothesis 3 concluded that all parameters reflect an expected association and are statistically significant except one variable (proportion of nonprofessional to total staff). Hence, this study could conclude that e-resource management is significantly affected by a vector of IT infrastructure facilities in the library. Hypothesis 4 concluded that there is no statistically significant association between groups of ranked libraries with different components of adoption of e-resource management. Hypothesis 5 concluded that no libraries present in management institutes in India have reported implementing ERMS.

7.15 SUGGESTIONS FOR IMPROVEMENT IN THE MANAGEMENT OF ELECTRONIC RESOURCES

1. Libraries should implement ERMS, which would entitle libraries to a number of benefits which have already been mentioned in Chapter 6.
2. Implementation of ERM requires skilled professionals. Therefore, it would be mandatory for existing library professionals to take ERM training on a regular basis.
3. All libraries should have dedicated e-resource managers to handle the task of ERM management efficiently. A dedicated e-resources manager should lead a team from different sections to implement ERM effectively.
4. It is essential to follow all the necessary steps and procedures involved within the lifecycle of an e-resource for better management.

5. Discovery or federated tools may be implemented for single search of all e-resources (purchase, subscribe, open source, or in-house) for better and more efficient management.

6. Mobile Apps should be developed for convenient access to and management of e-resources.

7. Cloud-based ERM should be adopted for a virtual web-based cost-effective service, which carries huge storage capacity along with high-end computing power, and convenient accessibility.

8. A dedicated dynamic website should be designed for easy retrieval of e-resources.

9. Integration of e-resources with ILMS/digital library software is essential in order to provide e-resources under one umbrella that can be accessed through OPAC.

10. It is recommended that the complete usage statistics data of e-resources is acquired before renewal. In order to generate effective usage statistic of e-resources, standards like "COUNTER" and "SUSHI" should be implemented.

11. Librarians (or e-resource managers) need to analyze the entire e-collections for effectiveness, cost-per-use, duplication of titles, and other analysis criteria that vary from institution to institution. In addition to this, they should be able to handle other administrative jobs, such as trial activation, IP registration, renewal, review license and exchange, report generation on different technical issues, and alerting services. On the other hand, end-users and service staff need to have information on permissions and restrictions for e-resource use.

12. Before subscription or purchase of e-resources, librarians (or e-resource managers) need to review each point of the license agreement meticulously.

7.16 AREAS FOR FURTHER RESEARCH

Lots of issues still remain unexplored and undiscussed in this area. This research has brought up some questions which need to be addressed for further development and management of e-resources in a library. This study mainly focuses on the investigation of the various procedures and systems that have been adopted in India for the management of e-resources, especially in management institutes. Following are some points for further research on e-resource management.

1. Management has two important perspectives: (1) the management professionals' perspective, and (2) the users perspective. User's satisfaction is an important component of management of e-resources. There is every need to understand the needs from the perspective of the user.
2. Researchers can be invited to examine "factors affecting e-resource management" in libraries.
3. How far are "library professionals" responsible for the better management of e-resources? How ready are the library professionals to adopt necessary technologies for better e-resource management?
4. Comprehensive research on electronic collections can be done to analyze cost − benefit, cost-per-use, title overlap, usage distribution, and worth of e-resources.
5. A similar kind of research may be carried out for other library types, such as technology, social science, scientific, and many more.

REFERENCES

[1] J. Vachhani, The impact of management education on executive's management effectiveness, Indian J. Appl. Res. 2 (3) (2012) 140−142.
[2] S. Johnson, O.G. Evensen, J. Gelfand, G. Lammers, L. Sipe, N. Zilper, Key Issues for E-Resource Collection Development: A Guide for Libraries, IFLA, The Netherlands, 2012, pp. 3−32.
[3] A. Field, Discovering Statistics Using IBM SPSS Statistics, 4th ed, Sage, London, 2013.
[4] D.N. Gujarati, Basic Econometrics, third ed., McGraw-Hill, New York, 1995.
[5] J. Emery, G. Stone, TERMS: techniques for electronic resource management, Library Technol. Rep. 49 (2) (2013) 5−43.
[6] S. Joshipura, Selecting, acquiring, and renewing electronic resources, in: H. Yu, S. Breivold (Eds.), Electronic Resource Management in Libraries: Research and Practice, Information Science Publishing, Hershey, 2008, pp. 46−65.
[7] R.O. Weir, Learning the basics of electronic resource management, in: R.O. Weir (Ed.), Managing Electronic Resources: A LITA Guide, ALA Techsource, Chicago, 2012, pp. 1−16.
[8] J. Poe, M. Bevis, J.B. Graham, B. Latham, K.W. Stevens, Sharing the Albatross of e-resources management workflow, in: H. Yu, S. Breivold (Eds.), Electronic Resource Management in Libraries: Research and Practice, Information Science, Hershey, 2008, pp. 71−89.

BIBLIOGRAPHY

[1] R. Alan, Electronic resource management: transition from in-house to in-house/vendor approach, Serials Librarian 47 (4) (2005) 17−25.

[2] B. Albitz, Licensing and Managing Electronic Resources, Chandos Publishing, Oxford, 2008.

[3] K.J.P. Anbu, S. Kataria, S. Ram, Dynamics of managing electronic resources: electronic resource management system (ERMS) initiatives, DESIDOC J. Library Inf. Technol. 33 (4) (2013) 300−305.

[4] K. Antelman, E. Lynema, A.K. Pace, Toward a 21st century library catalog, Inf. Technol. Libraries 25 (3) (2006) 128−139.

[5] B. Appleton, S. Regan, L. England, L. Fu, Improving Electronic Resources Management (ERM): Critical Work Flow and Operations Solution, Purdue University, Lafayette, Indiana, 2011.

[6] C. Armstrong, R. Lonsdale, A general overview of the e-resource industry, in: G. Stone (Ed.), The E-Resources Management Handbook, UKSG, Newbury, 2011, pp. 1−16.

[7] A. Bailey, G. Back, LibX−a Firefox extension for enhanced library access, Library Hi Tech 24 (2) (2006) 290−304.

[8] S. Bjorner, S.C. Ardito, Online before the internet, part 3: early pioneers tell their stories: Carlos Cuadra, Searcher. Searcher 11 (6) (2003) 36−46.

[9] K. Blake, J. Samples, Notes on operations creating organization name authority within an electronic resources management system, Library Resour. Techn. Serv. 53 (2008) 94−108.

[10] L. Blocker, Electronic resource management software: a brief overview, Tennesse Libraries 56 (3) (2006) 4.

[11] J.O. Borchers, Electronic books: definition, genres, interaction design patterns, in Conference on Human Factors in Computing Systems, CHI9 Workshop: Designing Electronic Books, 1999, April.

[12] S. Bordeianu, C.E. Carter, N.K. Dennis, Delivering electronic resources with Web OPACs and other Web-based tools: needs of reference librarians, Ref. Serv. Rev. 28 (2) (2000) 111−119.

[13] M. Breeding, The many facets of managing electronic resources, Comput. Libraries Westport 24 (1) (2004) 25−33.

[14] M. Breeding, Helping you buy: electronic resource management systems, Comput. Libraries 28 (7) (2008) 6−12.

[15] J.F. Brown, J.L. Nelson, M. Wineburgh-Freed, Customized electronic resources management system for a multi-library university: viewpoint from one library, Serials Librarian 47 (4) (2005) 89−102.

[16] T. Carpenter, B. McQuillan, O. Pesch, The three S's of Electronic resource management: systems, standards, and subscriptions, *NISO Webinars,* 2011.

[17] T. Carpenter, 2010. Standard columns, electronic resource management standardization: still a mixed bag.

[18] J.V. Caswell, Leveraging resources in a library gateway, Library Hi Tech 24 (1) (2006) 142−152.

[19] J. Caudwell, The fifth element: a symbiosis of cataloguing and metadata, The E-Resources Management Handbook, UK Serials Group (UKSG), Newbury, 2006, pp. 90−103.

[20] J. Chisman, G. Matthews, C. Brady, Electronic resource management, Serials Librarian 52 (3—4) (2007) 297—303.

[21] M. Collins, Electronic resource management systems (ERMS) review, Serials Rev. 34 (4) (2008) 267—299.

[22] M. Collins, J.E. Grogg, At ERMS length: evaluating electronic resource management systems, Library J. 136 (4) (2011) 22—28.

[23] A. Conyers, Usage statistics and online behaviour, The E-Resource Management Handbook, UK Serials Group (UKSG), Newbury, 2006, pp. 17—27.

[24] S. Corrall, The concept of collection development in the digital world, in: M. Fieldhouse, A. Marshall (Eds.), Collection Development in the Digital Age, Facet, London, 2012, pp. 3—25.

[25] S. Cukadar, A. Tuglu, G. Gurdal, New electronic resources management system for the ANKOS consortium, J. Acad. Librarianship 39 (6) (2012) 589—595.

[26] T.K. Das, Electronic information resource management in visva bharati library system: an overview, in Paper presented at the International Conference on Digital Libraries & Knowledge Organization-2011. Gurgaon, Haryana, 2011.

[27] C. Denholm, L. Kauler, J. Lavelle, L. Sokvitne, Making the new OPAC seamless: dealing with the transition from "finding" to "getting", Library Hi Tech 27 (1) (2009) 13—29.

[28] C.G. Doe, A look at web-based databases and search tools, Inf. Today, Inc 11 (5) (2004).

[29] W. Doering, G. Chilton, A locally created ERM: how and why we did it, Comput. Libraries 28 (8) (2008) 6—48.

[30] E.F. Duranceau, C. Hepfer, Staffing for electronic resource management: the results of a survey, Serials Rev. 28 (4) (2002) 316—320.

[31] A.C. Elguindi, K. Schmidt, Electronic Resource Management: Practical Perspectives in a New Technical Services Model, Chandos, Oxford, 2012.

[32] M. Ellingsen, Electronic resource management systems, LIBER Quart. 14 (3/4) (2004) 313—321.

[33] J. Emery, G. Stone, TERMS: techniques for electronic resource management, Library Technol. Rep. 49 (2) (2013) 5—43.

[34] J. Emery, Beginning to see the light: developing a discourse for electronic resource management, Serials Librarian 47 (4) (2005) 137—147.

[35] J. Emery, Ghosts in the machine: the promise of electronic resource management tools, Serials Librarian 51 (3—4) (2007) 201—208.

[36] J. Feather, R.P. Sturges, International Encyclopedia of Information and Library Science, Taylor & Francis, London, 2003.

[37] J. Feiler, Database-Driven Web Sites, Elsevier Science & Technology Books, Philadelphia, USA, 1999.

[38] T.A. Fons, T.D. Jewell, Envisioning the future of ERM systems, Serials Librarians 52 (1—2) (2007) 151—166.

[39] L. Galloway, Innovative interfaces' electronic resource management as a catalyst for change at glasgow university library, Serials Librarian 51 (1) (2006) 83—94.

[40] V.L. Gregory, A. Hanson, Selecting and Managing Electronic Resources: A How-to-do-it Manual for Librarian, Neal-Schuman Publishers, New York, 2006.

[41] J.E. Grogg, Electronic resource management systems in practice, J. Elect. Resour. Librarianship 20 (2) (2008) 86—89.

[42] D. Grover, T. Fons, The innovative electronic resource management system: development partnership, Serials Rev. 30 (2) (2004) 110—116.

[43] Y. Han, Digital content management: the search for a content management system, Library Hi Tech 22 (4) (2004) 355—365.

[44] E. Hartnett, A. Price, iPotential: mobile electronic resource management on an iPad, Library Collect. Acquis. Techn. Serv. 35 (4) (2011) 118—128.

[45] T.A. Harvell, Electronic resources management systems: the experience of beta testing and implementation, Serials Librarian 47 (4) (2005) 125–136.

[46] D. Hawthorne, J. Watson, Electronic resource management systems: alternative solutions, in Paper presented at *World* Library and Information Congress: 73rd IFLA General Conference and Council (pp. 19–23), 2007, August.

[47] G. Hodge, Preservation of and permanent access to electronic information resources: a system perspective, Inf. Ser. Use 25 (1) (2005) 47–57.

[48] G. Hodge, Metadata for electronic information resources: from variety to interoperability, Inf. Servi. Use 25 (1) (2005) 35–45.

[49] K.L. Horny, Online catalogs: coping with the choices, J. Acad. Librarianship 8 (1) (1982) 14–19.

[50] FLA, ISBD(ER): International Standard Bibliographic Description for Electronic Resource, Revised from the ISBD (CF): International standard bibliographic description for computer files, 1999.

[51] T.D. Jewell, A. Mitchell, Electronic resource management: the quest for systems and standards, Serials Librarian 48 (1–2) (2005) 137–163.

[52] T.D. Jewell, I. Anderson, A. Chandler, S.E. Farb, K. Parker, N.D. Robertson, Electronic Resource Management. The Report of the DLF Initiative, Digital Library Federation, Washington, DC, 2004.

[53] T. Jewell, J. Aipperspach, I. Anderson, D. England, R. Kasprowski, B. McQuillan, A. Riggio, Making Good on the Promise of ERM: A Standards and Best Practices Discussion Paper, NISO, Baltimore, 2012.

[54] T. Jewell, T.L. Davis, D. Grover, J.E. Grogg, Mapping license language for electronic resource management, Serials Librarian 52 (1–2) (2007) 29–36.

[55] T. Jewell, DLF Electronic Resource Management Initiative, Phase II: Final Report, Digital Library Federation and Council on Library and Information Resources, Washington, DC, 2008.

[56] S. Johnson, O.G. Evensen, J. Gelfand, G. Lammers, L. Sipe, N. Zilper, Key Issues for E-resource Collection Development: A Guide for Libraries, IFLA, 2012, pp. 3–32.

[57] A. Jose, Evaluation of digital libraries: a case study. ICSD-2007, 229-23, 2007.

[58] R. Kasprowski, Recent developments in electronic resource management in libraries, Bull. Am. Soc. Inf. Sci. Technol. 32 (6) (2006) 27–29.

[59] R. Kasprowski, Standards in electronic resource management, Bull. Am. Soc. Inf. Sci. Technol. 33 (6) (2007) 32–37.

[60] R. Kasprowski, T.T.A. Fons, T. Koppel, N.D. Robertson, Standards in electronic resource management, Proc. Am. Soc. Inf. Sci. Technol. 43 (1) (2006) 1–3.

[61] K. Kempf, Collection development in the digital age, JLIS 4 (2) (2013) 267–273.

[62] C.S. Kim, N.J. Cecchino, H.A. Harden, K.A. Danko, B.M. Koehler, Implementation of subject-accessible electronic resources through WELMA: the Welch electronic resource management system, J. Elect. Resour. Med. Libraries 1 (2) (2004) 57–67.

[63] S. Kumar, M.K. Dash, Management education in India: trends, issues and implications, Res. J. Inter. Stud. 18 (1) (2011) 16–26.

[64] M. Lebert, A short history of Ebooks, 2009.

[65] A.A. Lupton, M.K. Salmon, MULER: building an Electronic Resource Management (ERM) solution at York University, J. Library Innovat. 3 (2) (2012) 105–122.

[66] D.P. Madalli, Quality management in collection development of electronic resources, DRTC Workshop Inf. Manag. (1999) 1–16.

[67] R.P. Majumder, S. Roy, E-journals license and agreements: Some issues and practical overview, *Digital Media and Library Information services*, in Paper presented at the XXVI all India conference of IASLIC, Dr. Zakir Husain Library (Central Library), Jamia MilliaIslamia, New Delhi. 370, 2007.

[68] S. Mangrum, M.E. Pozzebon, Use of collection development policies in electronic resource management, Collection Building 31 (3) (2012) 108−114.

[69] E. McCracken, Description of and access to electronic resources (ER): transitioning into the digital age, Collection Manag. 32 (3−4) (2007) 259−275.

[70] T.M. McGeary, J.C. Hartman, Electronic resource management: a multi-period capital budgeting approach, Eng Econ 51 (4) (2006) 325−346.

[71] S. Meyer, Helping you buy: electronic resource management systems, Comput Libraries 25 (10) (2005) 19−24.

[72] S. Meyer, E-matrix: choosing to grow your own electronic resource management system, Serials Rev. 32 (2) (2006) 103−105.

[73] A.M. Mitchell, E is for entropy: electronic resource management systems, Serials Librarian 51 (3−4) (2007) 31−37.

[74] D. Murdock, Relevance of electronic resource management systems to hiring practices of electronic resources personnel, Library Collect., Acquis. Techn. Serv. 34 (1) (2010) 25−42.

[75] A. Murray, Electronic resource management 2.0: using Web 2.0 technologies as cost effective alternatives to an electronic resource management system, J. Elect. Resour. Librarianship 20 (3) (2008) 156−168.

[76] J. Musser, T. O'Reilly, Web 2.0: Principles and Best Practices, O'Reilly Media, Sebastopol, CA, 2007.

[77] W. Neubauer, A. Piguet, The knowledge portal, or the vision of easy access to information, Library Hi Tech 27 (4) (2009) 594−601.

[78] T.E. Nisonger, Electronic journal collection management issues, Collection Building 16 (2) (1997) 58−65.

[79] N.K. Patra, B. Kumar, A.K. Pani, Progressive Trends in Electronic Resource Management in Libraries, IGI Global, Hershey, PA, 2014, pp. 1−280. Available from: http://dx.doi.org/10.4018/978-1-4666-4761-9.

[80] O. Pesch, Usage statistics: about COUNTER and SUSHI, Inf. Serv. Use 27 (4) (2007) 207−213.

[81] R. Prytherch, Harrod's Librarians' Glossary and Reference Book, 9th ed., Gower, London, 2000.

[82] P.P. Rani, J. Geetha, Electronic resources in the modern libraries: a new path, in Paper presented at the 5th International CALIBER -2007, Punjab University, Chandigarh, 2007, February.

[83] C.A. Ruttenberg, Finding the tool that fits best: cloud based task management for electronic resources, OCLC Syst. Serv. 29 (3) (2013) 151−160.

[84] T. Sadeh, M. Ellingsen, Electronic resource management systems: the need and the realization, New Library World 106 (5/6) (2005) 208−218.

[85] G.G. Saha, Management education in India: issues and Concerns, J. Inf. Knowl. Res. Business Manag. Admin. 2 (1) (2012) 35−40.

[86] K.G. Saur, in: K.G. Saur (Ed.), ISBD(ER): International Standard Bibliographic Description for Electronic Resource: Revised From the ISBD(CF), International Standard Bibliographic Description for Computer Files, Vol. 17, UBCIM Publications, Washington, DC, 1997.

[87] M. Seadle, Selection for digital preservation, Library Hi Tech 22 (2) (2004) 119−121.

[88] R.K. Sharma, E-resource availability and importance for higher education and research in India, Learn. Commun. Internat. J. Educat. Soc. Dev. (1) (2011) 35−42.

[89] K. Silton, T. Lemaistre, Innovative interfaces electronic resources management system: a survey on the state of implementation and usage, Serial Rev. 37 (2) (2011) 80−86.

[90] A.P. Singh, M.T.M. Khan, S.K. Chauchan, Electronic resource management: emerging key issues. 5th International CALIBER -2007 (pp. 589−598), 2007.

[91] C. Smith, Electronic Resource Management Systems : The Impact of DLF ERMI Standards (2006) 1−20.

[92] M.G. Sreekumar, Strategies on e-resources management for smart information systems, Ann. Library Inf. Stud. (ALIS) 59 (3) (2012) 155−169.

[93] G. Stachokas, Managing electronic resources accessible, in: Ryan O. Weir (Ed.), Managing Electronic Resources: A LITA Guide, ALA TechSource, Chicago, 2012, pp. 69−85.

[94] S. Sukula, Electronic Resource Management: What, Why and How, Ess Ess Publications, New Delhi, 2010.

[95] P. Sullenger, A. Mitchell, Electronic resource management and the MARC record: the road less traveled, Serials Librarian 46 (3−4) (2004) 275−280.

[96] A. Taranum, XML and electronic publishing, Workshop Multimedia Int. Technol. (2001) 1−10.

[97] A. Thunell, L. Robinson, Conventional language for cataloging remote access electronic resources: the time is now!, OCLC Syst. Serv. 20 (3) (2004) 128−133.

[98] B. Tijerina, D. King, What is the future of electronic resource management systems? J. Elect. Resour. Librarianship 20 (3) (2008) 147−155.

[99] L. Tull, Electronic resources and Web sites: replacing a back-end database with innovative's electronic resource management, Inf. Technol. Libraries 24 (4) (2013) 163−169.

[100] L. Tull, J. Crum, T. Davis, C.R. Strader, Integrating and streamlining electronic resources workflows via innovative's electronic resource management, Serials Librarian 47 (4) (2005) 103−124.

[101] R. Turner, The vital link: the role of the intermediary in e-resources, The E-Resources Management Handbook, UK Serials Group (UKSG), Newbury, 2006, pp. 28−38.

[102] J. Vachhani, The impact of management education on executive's management effectiveness, Indian J. Appl. Res. 2 (3) (2012) 140−142.

[103] N. Verhagen, Licensing and negotiating: exploring unfamiliar ground, E-Resour. Manag. Handbook 1 (2006) 39−46.

[104] J.E.N.N.Y. Walker, New resource discovery mechanisms, The E-Resources Management Handbook, UK Serials Group (UKSG), Newbury, 2006, pp. 78−89.

[105] P.M. Webster, Managing Electronic Resources: New and Changing Roles for Libraries, Chandos, Oxford, 2008.

[106] F. Weigel, Taming the tiger technologically: through the standards jungle (and out again unscathed!), in: P. Bluh, C. Hepfer (Eds.), Managing Electronic Resources: Contemporary Problems and Emerging Issues, ALCTS Publishing, Chicago, 2006, pp. 78−90.

[107] J. Weintraub, Usage statistics at Yale university library: a case study, in: P. Bluh, C. Hepfer (Eds.), Managing Electronic Resources: Contemporary Problems and Emerging Issues, ALCTS Publishing, Chicago, 2006, pp. 100−109.

[108] R.O. Weir, Learning the basics of electronic resource management, in: R.O. Weir (Ed.), Managing Electronic Resources: A LITA Guide, ALA Techsource, Chicago, 2012, pp. 1−16.

[109] K. Wikoff, Electronics Resources Management in the Academic Library: A Professional Guide, Libraries Unlimited, Santa Barbara, California, 2012.

[110] D.E. Williams, K.A. Plummer, F.J. Bove, Tech services on the web, Tech. Serv. Quart. 25 (4) (2008) 95−102.

[111] K. Wilson, Electronic journal forum beyond library software: new tools for electronic resources management, Serials Rev. 37 (2011) 294−304.

[112] J. Wrosch, Using open source to provide remote patron authentication, Library Hi Tech 23 (4) (2005) 520–525.

[113] H. Yu, S. Breivold, Electronic Resource Management in Libraries: Research and Practice, IGI Global, Hershey, PA, 2008, pp. 1–440. Available from: http://dx.doi.org/10.4018/978-1-59904-891-8.

[114] P. Yue, L. Burnette, M. Howard, Betting a strong hand in the game of electronic resource management, Serials Librarian 54 (3–4) (2008) 207–209.

INDEX

Note: Page numbers followed by "*f*" and "*t*" refer to figures and tables, respectively.